Guys

ALSO BY WILLIAM THOMAS

The Tabloid Zone: Dancing with the Four-Armed Man
Malcolm and Me: Life in the Litter Box
Hey! Is That Guy Dead or Is He the Skip?

Guys

NOT REAL BRIGHT—
AND DAMN PROUD OF IT!

WILLIAM THOMAS

ILLUSTRATIONS BY TOM BANWELL

Stoddart

Published in 1996 by
Stoddart Publishing Co. Limited
34 Lesmill Road
Toronto, Canada
M3B 2T6
Tel. (416) 445-3333
Fax (416) 445-5967

Stoddart Books are available for bulk purchase for sales promotions, premiums, fundraising, and seminars. For details, contact the **Special Sales Department** at the above address.

Canadian Cataloguing in Publication Data

Thomas, William J., 1946-
Guys: not real bright — and damn proud of it!

ISBN 0-7737-5831-3

1. Men – Humor.   2. Canadian wit and humor (English).*
I. Title.

PS8589.H471G88 1996   C818'.5402   C96-931241-5
PR9199.3.T56G88 1996

Cover Design: Bill Douglas @ The Bang
Cover Photograph: Monica Rose

Printed and bound in Canada

Stoddart Publishing gratefully acknowledges the support of the Canada Council and the Ontario Arts Council in the development of writing and publishing in Canada.

FOR RED

An exceptional average guy

Contents

PART III Non-Excellent Adventures

PART IV Politicians: How Come They Never Listen to Me?

PART V Out of the Mouths of Men (and a Few Women, and a Couple of Kids) . . . Almost Too Weird for Words

PART VI Geeks "R" Us

Introduction

Years ago while I was writing a magazine profile of a crusty, ninety-year-old lawyer who was still practising, John Flett pointed a bony and bent finger at me and said, "Son, never trust the human mind in a crisis!"

John called me son even though I was thirty-eight at the time.

John was quite a sailor and had once survived a night on a cold and windy Lake Erie, clinging to his capsized boat.

"I was sailing off Point Abino," he began, "when a gale-force wind came out of nowhere and hit that sailboat broadside knocking my wife — my second wife — right into the drink!

"There we were, me trying to keep that boat from going over, her bobbing up and down between the rollers . . . And do you know what I did, son?"

"No," I answered.

"I turned that sailboat around and picked her up! *Never, ever* trust the human mind in a crisis, son. It's liable to do damn near anything!"

That's not the reason I've written this book. That's the reason I'm not crazy about sailing and I'm always leery of lawyers.

The reason I've written this book is because I have, I believe, a keen eye for the obvious as well as a uniquely critical appreciation of guys.

Readers of my weekly humour column send me things, stories and newspaper clippings about the strange goings-on of people, mostly men, confused, middle-aged, misguided men struggling to survive in a world that keeps nipping at their heels and sometimes bites them in the ass.

This is a book about the amazing, albeit bizarre, accomplishments of guys. This is a collection of stories that celebrate the fantastic feats of men. As I boasted to my publisher at the outset of this project, I am so uniquely qualified to write this book, so incredibly close to this fascinating subject, I can actually smell the feats of men.

Once on a Queen Street trolley car in Toronto, I shared the front side seat with two guys straight out of *Wayne's World*. In fact, listening in on their conversation, I learned that the one with the really long hair was named Garth. They hunched together in such a way that they could take intermittent swigs from bottles of Labatts Blue without the driver seeing them. They were pissed and it was eleven o'clock in the morning. Every time the trolley car shuddered or stopped or started up, they'd spill a bit of beer, curse softly, and shoot the driver a dirty look like she was doing it on purpose.

I don't remember what they talked about, except they used "party" as a verb a lot.

When the driver called out Yonge Street, they stashed the bottles in their plastic shopping bags and staggered down the steps, where they ran right into their buddy Ray, who was about to board the car. They did high fives, a secret handshake, and made plans to meet later, while passengers on each side of them waited for them to move. As Ray began to step up into the car, Garth grabbed his arm and with this genuine look of concern he said, "Ray, I wouldn't get on if I were you. She's all over the !*@%*' road with that thing!"

Garth didn't mean to make a joke, Ray didn't laugh, and nobody got it but me.

I am the sole messenger of such memorable accounts of men. As an earlier messenger said to Job in the Bible, "I only am escaped alone to tell."

The average guy, by definition, is neither the brightest nor the best society has to offer. I think we should be proud of our exploits, such as they are, and it's high time we stopped apologizing for our follies.Occasionally what we need is someone like Forrest Gump to read us our rights: "Men, you have the right to remain stupid."

We don't need your respect and we're not looking for pity. We want a couple of aspirin and something that will make us look less sheepish.

It's not as easy as it looks, being an average guy. No, sir. Just try walking a kilometre in our loafers and see if the shine is still on the penny. If you know what I mean.

PART I

The Middle-Aged Stupid Straight Guy Association

Men of the '90s, Unite! And Then Run Like Hell

LIFE AFTER THE SLICE HAS NOT BEEN EASY FOR GUYS.

Besides worrying about Ginsu knives stashed in the headboard of his bed, a middle-aged guy in the '90s has to worry about the sunburn he got two decades ago, hair loss, plaque, global warming, spousal swarming, movie popcorn, high cholesterol, low sperm count, the Jays' bullpen, olestra, downsizing, cartilage damage, his mother's home-care, alcohol intake, natural gas explosions, the long-term effects of tap water, short-term memory loss, impotence, his prostate, his Web site, his eyesight, and, finally, butt cleavage, now that his favourite pair of blue jeans has turned twenty years old.

It ain't easy being a male approaching the millennium, as witnessed by the far greater numbers of men undergoing sex-change operations than women surgically joining the male membership. (If you know what I mean.)

(Writer's note: Please understand that Robert Scott Cheuvrant's little escapade in Lakeland, Florida, was neither typical male behaviour nor an attempted sex-change operation. You may have read a newspaper story recently in which Robert, thirty-three years old, was observed standing at the shallow end of the Scottish Inn's pool from 12:30 A.M. until 4:30 A.M. Police were called and subsequently paramedics. The paramedics used an industrial lubricant to free Robert from the suction hole of the pool's filtration system. Relax, you have nothing to fear personally because it's a proven fact that men who sexually assault swimming pools are not all that attracted to living beings. There's also no indication whatsoever that Robert went around jail bragging about it later, saying things like, "Yeah, four hours straight and that pool was begging for more, man." You probably never thought you'd live in a world in which one day you'd have to use the plastic cover to save the virginity of your backyard swimming pool. I know, it's scary. But sit back and relax. I'm not from the government, but I am here to help.)

What's more frightening these days is seldom one man but a bunch of guys getting together for a common purpose other than knocking the snot out of a Third World country like Iraq.

Men used to band together for primarily two reasons: to make war or to move a fridge. Back in the '70s, when I was playing fastball in Welland, Ontario, I knew guys — namely Howie Doan, Al Chernish, and Gerry Maney — who would begin to move a beer fridge almost every Saturday morning and end up going directly to work Monday morning from the last basement their wives failed to search. I wasn't alone in suspecting that during all those years, it was the same fridge being moved.

Several years ago, Robert Bly, in his book, *Iron John*, extolled the benefits of men gathering together in the wilderness to find their "inner warrior." In America, men running around in the bush, dancing around fires, and chanting "Ay-o-yo-yo-yo-yo" was heralded as the new men's movement. In Canada, we were already tired of it and it was called Oka.

When guys found out that these wilderness weekends did not include Lite beer, the movement died.

Today in America, a million men march on Washington, D.C., to deliver a message of social dissatisfaction, while others just whip out a machine gun and strafe the White House.

Today in Canada, men come together as brothers, not just to strike for higher wages but also to raise the game of guydom to a higher level. At least that was the general idea on February 9, 1995, a day that was supposed to be a momentous occasion in the evolving history of the North American male.

The scene was carefully set: hundreds of rooms were booked, and press releases and speeches adorned the rows of seminar tables topped with jugs of ice water and goblets in the conference centre of Toronto's downtown Holiday Inn.

The guest speaker from Geneva, understandably nervous, took deep breaths in the wings, for this was the premier global gathering of Western males. Their mission: to explore and express their innermost feelings. This was the world's first-ever International Men's Day.

Five guys showed up. Honest.

Now, before you start snickering and reminding us men that five women show up at the fragrance demonstration station every ten seconds the Eaton Centre is open, I say sit down and listen, dammit.

Thank you.

So five men may not seem like a big crowd for an international convention, but you put that many men on the largest Harley-Davidson on the market and you're still at least three guys over the legal limit. Remember, five men in snowsuits constitutes two and a half Olympic bobsled teams. And five guys hurling down the ice shute on a luge means it's time to close the pub in the Olympic Village.

Now, there's some very legitimate reasons why, after a year of planning, and with every male in the universe eligible to attend, the total turnout was such that they could all enjoy lunch out of the same brown bag.

Organizers expected a turnout of 5,000, and there's no doubt in my mind that 5,000 well-intentioned males set out to attend this convention. Unfortunately, 4,995 are still out there driving around because they refused to stop and ask for directions to the downtown Holiday Inn.

Second, I don't think the theme of the conference was well presented. The organizers invited men, mostly from North America, to come and talk about their inner feelings, their oppressed state in society, male rights, and gender politics.

They should not have been quite so specific or descriptive. Men are easily confounded by too much information. For example, they would have sold out every hotel room in Toronto and nearby Hamilton if they had just asked North American men to come and express their feelings about, say, the baseball strike.

And it would have helped to put the date, time, and address of the convention on the front of T-shirts. And upside down for easy referral. Frankly, I believe some men were scared off by the "inner feeling" stuff. They imagined darkened rooms, jungle music, naked men dancing like animals and screaming war cries in search of the warrior within.

In fact, that's exactly what was happening at the Canadian Airborne Regiment's reunion across the street, where this year's theme was Searching for Your Inner Idiot. Military brass managed to trap themselves in the hotel's elevators for the entire weekend so they could later testify at public inquiries that they had no idea what was going on.

Now, as you know, women would turn out in droves to spend a weekend talking about their inner feelings, social status, etc. But for men, it must be in the form of a contest. We need to compete. We need the chance to win; we need to feel the fear of failure. A man can't sit through a two-minute Preparation H commercial without eventually rooting for the hemorrhoids. So if the organizers had billed the event as a game — say, men's inner warriors against the Golden State Warriors — bleacher seating would have been required.

Also, if they had replaced the ice water with jugs of complimentary draft beer, they could have filled the convention hall with walk-in traffic from the street. Throw in nachos and hot salsa and the organizers would have needed water cannons to control the overflow.

I think the planners of this forum assumed way too much. They assumed, for instance, that the average guy has an opinion. The fact of the matter is, if it weren't for bumper stickers and baseball caps, most of us would have nothing to say at all.

Communicate with other humans? Men? A man will talk to his dog, talk to his cat, talk to his TV, talk to himself. But when he wants to communicate with his spouse, he writes it on a napkin and sticks it on the door of the fridge with magnetic broccoli.

Sure, go ahead and say it: we're not that bright. Okay. But don't for a moment think we're not damn proud of it. If you look around at the world in which we live, knowing that men, almost exclusively, are responsible for its present state, and this makes you want to spew your stew, fair enough. But everything is relative. I mean, if you weigh what men have accomplished against women's expectations of us — hey! we're not doing too bad, are we?

I don't mean to get testy, but if there's one thing we understand perfectly, it's our limitations. That and math.

Calculating that there were approximately 75 million adult males in North America eligible to attend the first-ever International Men's Day Conference, and coming to the bottom line that five out of 75 million actually showed up to publicly discuss their inner feelings, we think that ratio is just about right. Tell other men about our most private thoughts? Yuck! It would be like reliving our first spin-the-bottle party and getting girl germs all over our faces.

Don't misunderstand me. It's not as if, as guys, we don't experience affectionate feelings, impassioned hopes, heartfelt fears. No, sir.

Sometimes when we least expect it, we will be absolutely overwhelmed by these warm and fuzzy feelings from within. We just hope like hell they're not permanent.

The Middle-Aged Stupid Straight Guy Association. You can just call us The Scare Club for Men.

(Postscript: In July 1995, the Second Annual International Men's Conference, held in Ottawa, was attended by 150 men who paid $350 each to register. This was a vast improvement over the first conference. Why? The organization of the Ottawa conference was contracted out to two women. This is absolutely true.)

Why Guys Are the Great Decision-Makers

*S*OMEWHERE AROUND THE TIME *JURASSIC PARK* WAS RELEASED, I REALIZED I was a dinosaur.

I do not own a computer or a word processor. I write long-hand on a clipboard. I do not own a fax machine. To file my scripts and columns, I first get them typed by Karen, my secretary, then drive to the local newspaper and use their copying and faxing facilities while the staff is distracted making personal phone calls on company time.

Last week I priced a fax machine, but the one I can afford doesn't make a bonded copy. Hence, I need a copy machine to go with it. To get a complete picture, I listed all the machinery required to literally beam me into the electronic age. Then I added up all the costs and did some creative financing to secure the money. (Thank goodness my mom still thinks IOUs are negotiable at the bank.)

And yesterday, with all the detailed information required to make an intelligent decision, I took the plunge. I did it. I bit the bullet. I did what I've been putting off doing for the last ten years. I bought a 1991 Special Edition Miata convertible, British racing green with leather interior, power windows, CD player, and speakers in the headrest. Honest, I did.

Simply put, it's the stupidest freakin' thing I've done since I voted for Brian Mulroney in 1984. (The only difference is, if the car turns out to be a lemon, I can always get rid of it, eh?)

I don't know what the hell got into me. I'm sitting at my desk totalling up the list prices of all that office equipment and I'm doing it on my fingers because I don't own a calculator. The figures keep getting steeper and then I remember I have to add on GST, so I'm cleaning the lint out from between my toes because now I'm getting into double

digits, when a guy by the name of Casey Clomp (I know, it gets weird-er by the minute) calls and says he's got the car I've been dreaming about and he mentions the price.

Now I know you're not going to believe this, but when I looked at the figure I had written on the top of my foot and the one I had in my ear, I nearly gave myself whiplash. Because even when I included shipping, freight, gas tax, and dealer prep, objects in the mirror were a lot closer than they appeared.

So I bought the car. And about an hour after I got the car home to Wainfleet, Casey called to tell me a Hamilton doctor has spotted it on the lot that morning on his way to work. He offered me a thousand more than I'd paid for it that afternoon.

I asked for the guy's name and address. Casey, who knew how

long I'd waited and how much I wanted an original Special Edition Miata, was shocked. "You're going to flip the car just like that?" he asked.

"Oh, no," I said, "I'm not selling the car. I just want to drive by the guy's house fifty or sixty times. I hate rich guys."

I have no idea why I bought this car. It's the most impractical thing on four wheels.

I thought it must be male menopause, so I went to my desktop encyclopedia to see if I had the symptoms. Apparently, male menopause is characterized by fears — fears of the future, of financial status, of job loss. Whew! I got lucky there. I mean, if I don't have any of those things, how could I possibly fear them?

It's ridiculous. This car is so small, I cannot possibly take my family for a drive, ever again. Oh, sorry. That's actually the feature that sold me on the vehicle in the first place!

There is absolutely no room in the trunk for a piece of luggage or even a suit bag, which is fine because I hawked everything including the shirt off my back just to make the down payment.

And you know those nasty nuts and bolts and stones that trucks kick up on the highway and crack your windshield? Well, in a convertible they do the same thing to your forehead.

About the only practical advantage of this car is that it once and for all eliminates the backseat driver. No back seat!

No doubt about it, I still have to run into town to make a photocopy, and after 5 P.M. I have to bribe the girl at the local variety store to send a fax for me. As far as my day-to-day life is concerned, I'm still driving around like an idiot — but now I look pretty darn good doing it!

The Gemini Awards: The Limo Also Picks Up Losers

$\int$EVERAL YEARS AGO, I WAS NOMINATED FOR A GEMINI AWARD, IN THE category of Best Writing in a Comedy, Variety, or Performing Arts Program, for the television movie I scripted, *Breaking All the Rules — The Story of Trivial Pursuit*.

The Academy of Canadian Cinema and Television named four nominees for 1988. That I could be singled out for national recognition in the craft of writing will no doubt shock the hell out of most of you. I know my mother has never been quite the same since.

Most Canadians are not all that impressed by, or interested in, the Gemini Awards. A recent survey showed that 76 percent of Canadians believed a Gemini was actually the Honda Accord with a sunroof and factory air. The other 24 percent believed it was the island where Ernest Hemingway used to bone-fish. But when you come from Wainfleet and you've lived most of your life in a place called Dain City, a Gemini nomination is one big deal. For my family, it was like having our uncle Ranald's prison release take effect on Groundhog Day.

So, dressed to the nines, ten of us piled into a six-seater and headed for the Big T.O., as excited as all get out. So excited that by Winona, nature called on the cellular phone and we all got out. We looked like the Beverly Hillbillies when we checked into the Sutton Place Hotel in Toronto — cans of cocktail nuts bouncing on the lobby floor, beer coolers, kindling, a tent. The guy at the front desk must have been psychic because even before one of us flashed a credit card or mentioned a reservation, he said, "The party from Wainfleet, right?"

And party we did. In the stretch limo provided by the academy, we pushed and pulled every visible knob and we kept referring to Mom as Miss Hepburn so the driver would think we were important.

At the very regal Constitution Hall in the Metro Toronto Convention Centre, we put one of the four cash bars out of business by 7 P.M. with our enthusiastic patronage. Inside the hall, where swirling searchlights and elaborate floral arrangements dazzled the one thousand formally attired guests, the meal was so good and so plentiful, we didn't even get through half the stuff we'd brought in picnic baskets. We weren't all that bad. When the master of ceremonies asked us to remove the sign on our table that read "Party Till You Pass Gas," we did so immediately.

And let me tell you, to be a nominee for a Gemini Award is an exhilarating experience. A ticket for your mom costs $165; the tux is $90; two days' parking in Toronto is several thousand dollars, provided you're out by 8 A.M.; a beer at the hotel bar is $4.85. And for all this you get to hear the desk sergeant on *Cagney & Lacey* not mention your name after he's ripped open the envelope and announced: "The winner is . . ."

I lost. I lost to Avrum Jacobson, who wrote the movie *Family Reunion*. It could have been worse. I could have lost to four guys who wrote *Blast From the Past*, a story about raccoons.

I lost early, so there was plenty of time to publicly sulk. And by losing, I avoided the trauma of an acceptance speech. I wasn't sure I could keep a grip on myself. I kept remembering the last time I'd broken down and cried — when I'd heard about that busload of lawyers that drove off a cliff, with four seats still vacant.

What was an otherwise pleasant evening for us all was marred when Avrum Jacobson passed by our table with his Gemini Award and my mother tried to bury her steak knife in his back. Most people in the hall didn't notice, because by then my friends were moving through the crowd leading them in the chant of "Fix! Fix! Fix!"

People from Wainfleet don't take losing lightly. Not at Toronto prices, we don't.

I may be guilty of embellishing the events of that night, but I swear this part is true. After I lost, there were heartfelt condolences all around the table and my mom gave me a big kiss and said I'd always be a winner in her book. (Hell, she's only got one son!) After it sunk in a bit, she turned to me in all seriousness and said: "Does this mean we don't get to take the limo back to the Sutton Place?"

No, Marg, even in the business of television they can't get the bad news out that fast. Provided it's same-day service, the limo also picks up losers.

As if my diet was still lacking humility, I was nominated for another Gemini last year, and of course, I lost again. This was in the category of Best Sports Program for co-producing *Chasing the Dream*, a documentary film on minor league baseball. I also wrote it. We lost — producers David Barlow, Peter Raymont, and myself — to a film entitled *Elvis Airborne*. Can you believe it? We lost to a movie about twenty-five Elvis impersonators parachuting out of an airplane over Las Vegas and landing safely in the parking lot of Caesar's Palace on top of George Foreman.

I'm kidding, of course. As you know, *Elvis Airborne* was the sad and revealing story of Elvis Presley, who was forced to serve in the U.S. Army at a base in Germany and, upon his arrival, he is hazed by troops from the Canadian Airborne Regiment and for the entire film they just keep eating the same cheeseburger over and over and over again.

The biggest winners at the 1995 Gemini Awards were *Due South*, *Road To Avonlea*, and *North of 60*. These aren't film titles! They're directions on a road map. You see, the judges of Canadian television programming are a bunch of lost souls. You can't just give them a title; you need to give them good directions on how to get to your story. There's no question in my mind we would have won the award with the title *Chasing the Dream on the Team Bus from Medicine Hat through St. Catharines, Across the Peace Bridge, and Over to Oneonta, New York*.

Actor David Gardner delivered a long but stirring tribute to the television writing of author Timothy Findley, who was the winner of the prestigious Margaret Collier Award. Then, with everybody about to lurch to their feet and burst into applause, he announced that Timothy Findley was in Australia and not able to accept the award personally.

This is wrong. This puts a damper on audience enthusiasm. They should do what guys do when they raffle off a bottle of rye at a stag. If the winner isn't there to claim the prize, they just pick another name. Gemini presenters should simply start shouting out seat numbers until they hit one with a writer's butt in it. Hell, I was there all night. I had an acceptance speech I wasn't using.

I may have appeared a little too anxious to win a Gemini that night. I was sitting next to Terry Steyn when he won the Gemini for Best Short Dramatic Program with *Something to Cry About*. When Terry returned to our table, I was overcome with emotion. I hugged him. I said, "I love you, man. And if we do nothing else in television ever again, we'll have this award to share for the rest of our lives."

Terry asked my friend David Barlow who I was and would he please help him get the Gemini out of my hands.

The lady I was with had a great time, too, but she didn't know a lot about the Gemini Awards.

The winning producer of *This Hour Has 22 Minutes* was so excited, he thanked everybody in Eastern Canada for his good fortune and ended his speech with a real Down East expression. Thrusting his Gemini high above his head, he claimed: "We'll be fartin' through silk tonight!"

My date turned to me with a very confused look on her face. Having been nominated before, I assured her this was not a Gemini tradition. If I won, I promised to find another way to celebrate, one that wouldn't cause the dogs in the neighbourhood to begin barking for no apparent reason.

Alas, it was not to be. I lost, and it could be years and years before I have another chance, years and years before I get to wear my hair in a ponytail, put on a black suit over a black T-shirt, and thank everyone including Enzo at my favourite ristorante for his delightful double decaf iced cappuccino.

In fact, that's my next film — *On the Road with Enzo, Due South Just North of Highway 60*. Bitter? Me?

As a Writer, You Gotta Have Fans

AS YOU'RE READING THIS, THE CHANCES ARE I'M BACK ON THE BOOK TOUR again.

For anybody who has written a book in this country, the promotional parade that follows is obligatory. You get to sit beside radio hosts who, having lost the copy your publisher sent them, say, "So, what's the book about, Bill?"

"It's about my career as Lady Di's riding instructor, Jack," I say, "and how I'm deathly afraid of horses."

Next question: "Were you always funny?"

Answer: "You know, Jack, I think I was because at the very beginning when the doctor slapped me, I was real tired from the journey and I couldn't even raise my arm to give him the finger. But my mother said I managed to moon him."

I used to be so naive, I assumed people who worked in the large chain bookstores read books. They don't, of course. They know about as much about their books as McDonald's employees know about what goes into their sausage patties. On the other hand, the independent bookstores are wonderful places for writers. They understand that you create the things they sell for a living. (They also really like the fact that as the writer, you earn 10 percent of the list price while they make 50 percent.) But the large chain bookstores have no idea who you are or why you're there, and they can never find those "Author Signed" cards to indicate autographed copies.

They also have a little problem with categories. I was amazed that my book *Malcolm and Me: Life in the Litter Box* became a bestseller in this country despite the fact that every chain bookstore buried it under "Nature."

Nature? *Malcolm and Me* is the story of a buck-toothed cat who was out the door every morning at eight to stalk the neighbourhood like a raging Bengal tiger and back in by ten to take a leak. Malcolm had more in common with a VCR than with nature.

So this upset me until I read that the chain bookstores placed W. O. Mitchell's last book, *The Black Bonspiel of Willie MacCrimmon*, under "Black Studies," and Douglas Gibson's book about genealogy, *In Search of Your Roots*, was strategically shelved in the "Gardening" section. I am not making this up.

On my last book tour, I was whining about all this in London, Ontario, as my publishing rep, Bob Coltri, ushered me around to the bookstores. Gentle Bob was sympathetic, but I got the feeling he thought I was exaggerating the disrespect writers get from the chain stores, just as we walked into one.

He introduced me to the manager and a sales clerk. They were pleasant.

The manager went to the back and returned with fifteen copies of my last book *Hey! Is That Guy Dead or Is He the Skip . . . Curling and Other Stories I Wish I'd Never Written*. Please understand, the cheap shot at curlers in the title was my publisher's idea. They turned down my perfectly kind and gentle curling title, "Curling: The Game for the '90s . . . (But You Gotta Be That Old to Enjoy It!)."

Standing at the counter, I duly autographed each copy of my book and stacked them neatly in front of me, next to the cash register. And as God and Bob Coltri are my witnesses, the sales clerk smiled at me sweetly and said, "Can I put those in a bag for you, sir?"

I did a quick study of Bob's face to see if he'd set me up. He hadn't.

"No, thanks," I said. "I wrote the damn thing. No need for me to read it over and over and over again fifteen times!"

It was also in London that I had the pleasure of being interviewed on CKSL radio by talk-show host Jim Chapman, a man of intelligence, humour, and modesty. Jim had read the book, and we had more fun in half an hour than ought to be legal for two straight guys.

After the interview, while we were racing from station to bookstore to interview, I ducked into a beer store for a six-pack I would need that evening.

On tour, the book never leaves your sight, so as I put it on the counter to fish out some cash, the kid at the register said, "Hey! I just heard that guy on the radio!"

Now I have to tell you honestly, unidentified bodies in the morgue have a higher recognition rating in Canada than writers. This was my moment. This was going to make the whole harried day worthwhile.

"Well," I said, savouring the moment and forcing a modest smile. "That guy is me."

The kid beamed, he took a step back, and with his hands raised expressively in front of him he said, "You gotta tell me . . . *What's Jim Chapman really like?*"

Saying I was deflated is like saying the *Hindenburg* was just a little late in arriving. I grabbed my beer, my change, and my book, and as I turned I yelled: "Jim Chapman is a cross-dressing, sadomasochistic, laughing loon who insists you wear a frilly nightgown when you do the show with him! I thought everybody in this town knew that!"

Jim — I'm sorry. I just hope you understand. I was angry.

And Jim, I was also in a hurry. The gown is in the mail, buddy.

Yes, the book tour for a writer can be a mortifying experience, but not the book signing. There's a big difference. The book signing for an author is the shrine to which the fans flock for a handshake and a scribbled signature. The book signing is an exercise in adoration complete with clever exchanges of wit and wisdom. Believe me, I know, because my friend Arthur Black tells me this happens to him all the time.

For me, a good signing is one at which the person who organized it actually shows up and I have somebody to talk to.

I've had a man in Midland ask me to inscribe two books "To Big Ears One" and "To Big Ears Two." (I checked. They were not his children!) I've had a woman in Niagara Falls bring half her *Malcolm and Me* book to me to sign — the half her dogs didn't eat. I've had a desperate last-minute shopper in Hamilton rush up to me and say, "I don't know who the hell you are, but I'm sure the wife'll be impressed. Sign it!" I'm sure she'll be impressed, too. You don't often find Boutros Boutros-Ghali's signature on a book about curling.

The typical setting for one of my book signings, as arranged by my publisher's publicist, would be — not a bookstore, not a library, not a chance — no, I sign books in places like Walt's Beanery, a restaurant/bar in Jackson's Square in downtown Hamilton, Ontario. Walt's motto is (I am not making a word of this up) "Try our beans and let us hear from you." Not having real good luck at book signings, I made a point to call ahead and request the no-smoking section.

But the worst book signing that ever took place was at an outdoor café on Bestor Plaza at the Chautauqua Institute in Western New York, where I teach for two weeks each summer. I had just left the lecture in the outdoor amphitheatre, where celebrated American cartoonist Jerry Robinson, creator of the Batman comic covers, was regaling the crowd with personal anecdotes. As I passed the Courtyard Café, Jim Rosselli of Jamestown's WJTN radio, who broadcasts a live talk show from the café's porch on summer mornings, appeared to be in trouble.

First, he kept looking at his watch like his guest was late, then he grabbed me as I walked by and yanked me into the booth. Jim, the consummate conversationalist, can get a good ten minutes out of an ashtray if he has to. I forget what we talked about — baseball, probably — but I do remember an older woman who looked like a retired schoolmarm, smiling and waving at me from the far end of the café's porch.

A roar went up in the amphitheatre, signalling the end of the lecture. Jim eased me out of the booth, which told me Jerry Robinson was his scheduled guest. I jumped on my bicycle to leave.

As I pedalled by the smiling lady, she raised a hand, and I stopped.

"I'm a very big fan of yours," she said. "Could I get your autograph?"

"Gee," I mumbled. "Are you sure you . . ."

"Oh, yes," she said. "I couldn't find any of your books in the bookstore." Well, the bookstore had stocked a few copies and they were now sold out.

"Well," I said, reaching into the bike's carrier where I had two copies of *Malcolm and Me*, "If you really want one, I have a copy here."

She was thrilled. I was dreaming of a green card. Americans! They know how not to treat writers.

As she put a $20 bill on the table, I signed and inscribed the book to her — "Lydea, with and E and an A."

She told me how she and her sister had driven up from Buffalo just to hear my lecture, but they were told it was sold out. Actually, you have to pre-register, but why quibble.

Still straddling my bike, I began to shove off, when she mentioned her sister would also love a copy.

Out came a $50 bill, back went a ten in change, to "Eanid, with an E and an A."

I was gracious, she was effusive. It was one of those moments in the sun, but the fact was the bicycle seat was killing me and I was late.

"One last question," she said. "When did you first begin to draw?"

I interrupt this story to bring you the three late-breaking bulletins that flashed across the bottom of the screen on my brain.

1. This woman had not heard a word of the radio interview or looked at the books she was now holding.

2. This woman thought I was the famous American cartoonist Jerry Robinson.

3. I would never, in my lifetime, find two sisters named Lydea and Eanid to sell these books to.

"Well," I said nervously, "I guess I was about four or five. But I wasn't very good at it."

"Oh," she said, giving me a small wave like I must be the most modest man on earth. "You artists!"

I know what you're wondering! The $50? Harry Chapin would be proud of me — I stashed the bill in my shirt.

As I pedalled off, I heard Jim Rosselli yell, "See you next summer, Bill." It was at that moment I sensed the sun went behind a cloud, but the heat on my back got hotter.

Fans! What would I be without them?

Killing a Spouse for a Book Deal Is Wrong!

O NCE IN A WHILE AT A WRITERS' WORKSHOP OR SEMINAR SOMEBODY WILL ask me about the best way to write a bestseller.

My standard answer is, tell a beautiful story, make 'em laugh, make 'em cry, and literary agents will stage a hostile takeover of your bathroom until you sign a contract.

But we tried that, they'll say, and it didn't work.

So create and tell a real grisly tale, I'll say, so horrific that readers will cringe and upchuck on the pages, after which Stephen King will accuse you of plagiarism.

And they'll say no, they don't want to make people sick.

So I'll say, okay, here's the deal: are you married? Yes? Then kill your spouse.

And they'll say, but I love that person, and I'll say perfect, because that will bring a genuine sense of remorse and raw emotion to your soon-to-be-released bestseller, *The Kind and Caring Killer — With an Introduction by Jean Harris*.

Call me naive, but back in 1978 when I was still married and beginning my career as a writer, it never once occurred to me that the best way to clinch a great book deal was to whack my wife. (That's not to say the idea didn't cross her mind more than once.)

Murdering-your-mate books generally follow one of two premises. There's the "I'm Guilty as Sin and Damn Sorry for It" approach, or the absolute denial in the face of overwhelming evidence, like *I Want to Tell You* by O. J. Simpson. Further denial can be published in video form, *The Interview*, at $29.95 a pop. Simpson made millions denying the obvious.

Over Nicole Brown Simpson's body, no fewer than seven people claiming to be a dear friend, innocent spouse, failed white prosecutor, failed black prosecutor, trash-talking defender, Robert "I said no to the race card" Shapiro, and even Alan "I also got Klaus von Bulow off!" Dershowitz will receive multimillion-dollar advances for writing books about something that everybody in this world saw on television and pretty much knows the ending.

As I write, not one, but two books based on RCMP officers who have killed their wives are on the way up the bestseller charts in Canada. And there's always Jean Harris, who shot and killed her lover, Herman Tarnower, the Scarsdale Diet Doctor, and then wrote two bestsellers: *Strangers in Two Worlds* and *They Always Call Us Ladies*. (I'm going way out on the limb here, but I'm betting the last thing Herman referred to Jean as did not include the word *lady*.)

You might recall that Jean Harris, before she ran up against some petty Canadian immigration officials who look down their noses at convicted killers, was scheduled to speak at Toronto's Roy Thomson Hall as part of the very prestigious women's series called "Unique Lives and Experiences." I can only imagine Jean Harris's unique experience came after she pumped three shots into ol' Herman and then stood there as he bled low-fat cottage cheese all over the carpet.

No, this killing of spouses for juicy material in order to write a bestseller just naturally has to stop. If you're married and you have aspirations of writing a book, remember that little phrase you both repeated at the altar: "till death do us part." This was never meant to be the beginning of the plot line.

Imagine you've just picked up his underwear for the umpteenth time, and you mumble to yourself, "Why, I could just kill . . ." Stop! Proceed immediately to the stain remover and fabric softener. Do not call a literary agent.

Sure you want to be a bestselling author, but remember, the life insurance policy you're holding on your spouse was never meant to be an advance against royalties. It's in case somebody dies *accidentally*. Nowhere does that policy use the terms *hero* or *heroine*.

And you certainly don't need Miss Manners to tell you that

conducting taped interviews at the funeral of your spouse is poor etiquette.

Recently, the business of bestsellers just took a nasty turn. Scientists at Georgia State University have taught a chimpanzee to write words with a computer keyboard. In no time at all, he mastered 200 words.

How long will it be before we're mourning the death of pop star Michael Jackson and reading promo ads for *I Killed the Little Crotch Grabber* by Bubbles the Chimp?

Please, killing a spouse for the sake of writing a book about it is wrong. Period.

On the other hand, if we're talking about a movie deal here, I still know where my ex lives.

I Have Seen the Future for Guys

THANK GOD FOR LABORATORY SCIENTISTS.

Think about it. Many of these people possess medical degrees. If it wasn't for cushy jobs in the lab and lucrative government grants, these people would take positions in hospitals and have surgical access to your body.

In the past year alone, laboratory scientists have come forth with such amazing advances in technology as wine on a stick, pop-top oysters, a car combustion system that runs on wine, a robot that milks cows, and an anti-depressant pill that causes quite a quiver in your knickers when you yawn. All true.

Wine on a stick? "Whaddayamean, I'm impaired? Ossiffer, all I had is eight popsicles for lunch. What the hell are they puttin' in those things, anyway?"

Wine in your gas tank? "Good morning, sir. Will that be unleaded or a pretentious little cabernet with a woody nose and an apricot finish?"

Wine in the gas tank will change tail-gate parties forever. No coolers, no corkscrews — you just lay out the food and drop a siphon hose down the tank of your car.

May I recommend the old Volkswagen Beetle, which has two gas tanks, allowing you to serve red with the beef-on-weck and white with the chicken salad.

In Holland, they've perfected a machine that, when activated by a chip in the cow's collar, approaches and then milks the animal. Said one researcher, "The cows tend to like it." Let's not overstate the situation. The cows tend to like it better than having their breasts groped and pulled by the cold hands of guys name Joop and Rude.

I will barely make mention of the U.S. researchers at Pacer Technologies who are seeking FDA approval of Rectite, their new super-glue that prevents salmonella contamination by — this is absolutely true — sealing the rectums of turkeys. In this case, it's highly unlikely you'll hear a researcher quoted as saying, "The turkeys tend to like it."

I'll say this: if the turkeys weren't already a little anal-retentive around Thanksgiving, they sure will be once a lab technician makes their pucker permanent with contact cement.

And the French (motto: In War, We Surrender; In Peace, We Detonate Nuclear Bombs) have come up with the pop-top oyster. This is a fresh oyster, shucked and encased in hard plastic with a pop-top tab for easy access. No doubt about it, after world peace, food for starving nations, and a cure for about fifty fatal diseases, what the world needs most is an oyster that opens like a can of Dr. Pepper.

The pop-top oyster comes very close to an invention of mine called speedy escargot. By surgically attaching a snail's reproductive organ to his lower colon and then applying heat from a steaming pot, the escargot actually gooses himself out of his shell in 2.5 seconds flat. It does nothing to improve the taste, but it's a lot more fun to watch than an oyster being slurped through an aluminum hole.

And by now, you've heard of clomipramine, the anti-depressant drug that causes patients to experience an orgasm whenever they yawn. Ain't modern medical technology grand? They finally come up with a cure for depression and the side effect is nymphomania. "Look, Ma! No hands!" Women on clomipramine no longer have to seek out exciting, virile men. No, now they can have a sexually fulfilling relationship with really boring guys . . . like dentists.

Of course, you see where all these advancements in technology are headed. There's no doubt in my mind that the global search for the "ultimate guy pill" is on, and they're getting very, very close.

The ultimate pill for guys will be called the Pearl and it will come in a pop-top oyster so there's absolutely no work involved in getting at it.

The oyster itself will serve as the aphrodisiac, heightening the anticipation for a guy's greatest pleasure — watching sports on television.

The Pearl will contain the following: a stimulant to keep him awake during the game, an appetite depressant to eliminate the need to go to the kitchen for pretzels, clomipramine so he can yawn and climax during the instant replays, nicotine so he doesn't have to light up a cigarette after he, ah, yawns, and Nytol, so he can roll over and go to sleep as soon as it's over.

Man's best friend, a dog-like robot with a chip in his collar, will bring the oysters and cold draft beer right to the couch.

If things get really dull, the dog robot can always be programmed to go out and milk a cow. Cows tend not to like this, but real farm dogs are very impressed.

Yes, I have seen the future for guys, and it's, like, awesome, eh?

Crash Test Dolls Could Save Your Life

BABY, THINK IT OVER IS A BRILLIANT INVENTION BY SAN DIEGO ENGINEER Richard Jumain.

This anatomically correct doll, which cries, screams, and pees without warning, just like a real baby, has social agencies in the United States ordering at a rate that far exceeds production.

The doll's erratic baby-like outbursts trigger an alarm that can be turned off only by a key. The idea is to have teenage girls who think it would be really neat to have a baby carry this little bundle of mayhem around for a month or so, sleep in the same room with it, and be ready at any moment to rush over with the key to restore peace, quiet, and dryness. The doll even has a monitor to register rough shaking or slapping, thus discouraging such behaviour.

After a month, the young women are asked, "Now, do you really want a baby?" The answer is almost always "I'll think it over."

And that's why I've launched a $10-million lawsuit against Richard Jumain for intellectual theft. You see, I've had this same basic idea for years. The only difference between my doll and Richard's is 200 pounds and a five-o'clock shadow. Otherwise, the concept is the same.

My doll is a six-foot-tall anatomically correct male that performs all the functions of a baby, except he can't cry. He never cries. If he cries, a group of other six-foot-tall anatomically correct males are standing by to point at him and laugh.

My doll has a bit of a paunch, thinning hair, and a six-pack strapped to the inside of the right foot so, when he sits down in front of the television set, the beer is right there on the floor where he can reach it.

My doll walks and talks, wears loose underwear and T-shirts with mustard stains, and he can make a scary noise like a foghorn, except you never see his lips move.

My doll can write his name in the snow. My doll's name is Hubby Think It Over.

A single woman, hoping someday to get married, carries Hubby around the house for one month. She pushes him out of bed in the morning, makes his meals, does his dishes, refills his six-pack, hands him the remote control, puts a pillow behind his head while he sleeps in front of the television, and eventually gets him into bed, where he performs his finest function — loud snoring.

At any time, night or day, she must run to him when she hears his alarm go off (a belch) and, using a special key, stop whatever male malfunction he may be performing at the time. She is not allowed to wear a blindfold.

At the end of one month, the woman does an easy two-step marriage evaluation. First, she honestly answers the question: Do I really want to get married? Then she begins memorizing the vows necessary for investiture into the Carmelite order of nuns.

I would have had Hubby Think It Over on the market the week major league baseball went on strike, but then I had to add a "rant and rave" feature. Also due to the baseball strike, Hubby Think It Over now cries. He cries almost every day. And the group of other guys cry so hard, it is questionable whether they're still anatomically correct.

As a companion product, I now have Honey Think It Over in development. The real problem I'm having is that the female doll overuses the cerebral mechanism and is always blurting out relevant questions like, "Do you still love me?" to which Hubby invariably replies, "Did you see that!?! He dropped that sucker like a three-foot putt!"

Honey is very hard to reprogram: "You used to love me, but I don't think you love me. Why can't we seem to communicate any more?"

Hubby begins to squirm and sweat, then tries to drink from the remote control and squeezes a can of beer until it explodes. "Ah, geeze," he says.

No matter how much I reduce the frequency, Honey blurts out: "What are you thinking about right now?"

"Ah, geeze," Hubby says, just before his head bursts into flames.

When I finally perfect Hubby and Honey, I'm going to give them away to customers free of charge. The keys that shut them off will cost $10,000 each.

Baby, Hubby, Honey — let's seriously think it over.

Guy Gifts for Christmas: Shopping Below the Belt

$\int$ TILL AT A LOSS IN FINDING THAT PERFECT GIFT FOR YOUR FAVOURITE GUY this Christmas?

Well, thanks to a marketing-mad world that puts hedonism far ahead of humanity, great guy gifts are available just in time to celebrate the birth of . . . the birth . . . it's probably not important, but I recall something about a religious event being associated with this time of year. Maybe I'm thinking of Easter.

Anyway, if you're tired of seeing your man dragging his ragged ass around the house — bingo! — Miracle Boost jeans for men. Get your hubby into a pair of Miracle Boost jeans and instantly that bum . . . sorry, that bum's bum will be higher, harder, and rounder than the SkyDome.

Yes, through the wonders of Spandex, your man can have buns of steel, so much so that when he walks through the kitchen, his rear end will rip all those tiny fruit magnets off the refrigerator door. If you want a man with buns so steely he sets off airport metal detectors before he even gets out of the car, these are the jeans for you. Miracle Boost jeans hold their form so well, a guy in the process of taking them off may, for a split second, perform the always-popular but ever-elusive "double moon."

You say you like the idea of a butt that doesn't remind you of sand bags, but you haven't been able to get your man to wear pants around the house since they came out with oversized gochees featuring cartoons of the Fruit of the Loom boys. No problem. Rush Industry of New York brings you Super Shaper briefs.

Made of foam-padded Spandex, these shorts give your hubby's haunches a rounder, firmer, more contoured look. Never again will your man have to turn the other cheek. Super Shaper briefs do both.

Super Shaper underwear is being advertised as the Wonder Bra for men. Call me old-fashioned, but I never thought I'd see the day when the words *lift and separate* pertained to my own rosy red hams. And the big bonus, so to speak? I swear this is true: an optional snap-in fly-front endowment pad for larger-than-life frontal size.

Trust me, this is not the endowment for the arts you've been hearing so much about.

No, the frontal endowment pad is designed to make a guy at a wedding look like he's the best man, even if he's the limo driver. The endowment pad — I think this may demonstrate the inflated value all men place on this particular part of the anatomy — costs $5 extra. I think a great way to advertise the combination sets of Super Shaper briefs and endowment pad would be a line like: "What you lose on the buns, you gain on the frankfurter!" (If you know what I mean.)

Warning: Wearing the Miracle Boost jeans along with the Super Shapers and the endowment pad could cause a serious rash as well as attracting phone calls from Boy George.

Also on the market this Christmas is an item called Butt Boosters, which I will not elaborate on because I find it frivolous. I'm waiting for next Christmas, when I'm sure the same company will come out with Butt Blasters — asbestos-lined boxer shorts for beer-drinking guys who eat a lot of burritos.

If you're done with denim and find cotton too common, Xandria's of California is here to tell you, "It's better with leather." Yes, for that special guy in your life whom you affectionately refer to as "that dirty dog," you can now buy a leather locking collar. I'm very pleased to tell you I don't know what the hell this thing is for. But a word of advice: If you ever do manage to get the collar and leash on him, don't let him outside, no matter how bad he's gotta go.

Xandria's also offers a men's chastity belt, cheap at $124.95 if you've always wanted to own a genuine leather oxymoron. And for less than $70 you can buy your guy a latex leather jock with adjustable rings and matching harness. (Trust me, you don't want to know!)

You may want to buy your man a few of the aforementioned leather products not so much for fashion but as a test of your persuasiveness. Take a look at your husband. Now think about it: if you can actually get this guy to dress up in a dog collar, a chastity belt, and all this other bowl-of-fruit-type paraphernalia, your chances of getting him to take the green garbage bag out to the curb just increased dramatically.

If you're averse to artificially enhancing your man's anatomy, might I suggest a more traditional gift. Try to come up with a special offering in the spirit of the holiday season. Try something with meaning, something that speaks of men, mission, and time — such as the O.J. watch with the two police cars chasing a white Bronco around the dial. It's only $30.

Merry Christmas, and remember: it's really a celebration of the birth of . . . or the anniversary of . . . I know it's a miracle. No, no not the Miracle Boost. It's . . . it's *some* kind of miracle. Miracle Whip! No, that's not it. Geez, I saw the manger in the mall just yesterday.

It'll come to me, I'm sure.

Men: We Have the Right to Remain Stupid

A T THIS TIME OF THE YEAR, THEY SEEM TO COME BY THE BUCKETFUL, THE amazing feats of men. In fact, I can smell the feats of men, the pungent odour of testosterone coming off the pages of my daily paper as if they'd used scratch-and-sniff newsprint. Guy season is upon us.

(Warning: Women, do not attempt to match the following extraordinary achievements of the stronger sex. You are neither physically nor psychologically equipped for such exploits.)

The season opened recently with a gunshot that killed an Asian gang member in Toronto's Chinatown. The man's name was Chanh Thong Vo, but according to the *Globe and Mail*, "he was better known on the streets of Chinatown as 'Tommy,' or 'No Wang Vo' because four years ago he accidentally shot off part of his penis with the .45-calibre handgun he kept stuffed down the front of his baggy blue jeans."

Ah, if it's a choice, I'll take "Tommy" any day. To avoid a truckful of really bad puns, I think we're all relieved this guy's name wasn't Richard.

In Honolulu, after being convicted of assaulting his girlfriend and sentenced to undergo anger-management training, Miguel Gonzales was beaten to death by his counsellor. I don't care what you say, when you provoke your anger-management counsellor to the point where he strangles you to death with his bare hands, you got an attitude.

According to the Tass news agency, a Russian, ice-fishing on a lake a hundred kilometres northwest of Moscow, caught a 70-centimetre pike. Showing off for his buddies, he picked the fish up and kissed it on the mouth. The pike immediately clamped down and locked its razor-sharp teeth on the man's nose. Frantic, the man screamed for help (in a very nasal voice) and his friends beheaded the fish. Even then the jaws could not be pried apart, and the man's nose had to be freed at a local hospital.

Tass does not describe the reaction of other patients while the man sat in the doctor's waiting room.

The zoologist in charge of the Jersey Wildlife Trust stumbled onto a real bad idea recently when he released the world's rarest falcon on a preserve off the coast of Mauritius, which also happened to be the same habitat in which he had released the world's rarest pigeon. Today, there is one less rare pink pigeon in the world, but a very content kestrel falcon. When he burps, pink feathers fly out of his mouth.

Lesson learned: falcons like their pigeons rare, a little on the pink side.

Staging *Ubu the Barbarian* at Peterborough's Arbour Theatre, a play described by a cast member as "rude and obnoxious," was not such a hot idea. Of the forty senior citizens in attendance, twenty-nine left after the first act. Much like the stage story from Los Angeles in which Pia Zadora, playing the lead in *The Diary of Anne Frank*, gave such an awful performance that during the scene in which Anne is hiding upstairs in a closet with the Nazis pounding on the front door, the audience stood up and yelled, "She's upstairs hiding in the closet."

And in Brunswick, Georgia, detectives picked up a suspect in a purse snatching minutes after it happened and returned him to the scene of the crime, informing him that he was going to have a face-to-face identification with the victim. They hauled him out of the cruiser and positioned him directly in front of the woman. There was a pause, then the suspect said, "Yup, that's the woman I robbed, all right." Okay, maybe he's just new at this.

And he wasn't the only one lately in need of a shoehorn to spring his foot from his mouth. Infuriated by the Gainers meat-packing company's new "pee-for-a-fee" policy in which Edmonton workers would have to fill out forms and then be docked pay for time spent in the washroom, union president Dan McGee said, "This rule is enough to make me puke!" Then, reconsidering, he added, "But then I'd have to fill out a sheet for that too!"

All this in a place where they produce our finest grade A meats.

Equally angry, and taking the bodily function metaphor to yet another level, Garfield Mahood, former director of the Non-Smokers Rights Association, said, "Having smoking sections in restaurants is like having urinating and non-urinating sections in swimming pools." Certainly points well taken, but Dan and Garfield are the last two guys you'd invite on a Saturday night pub crawl, unless you're wearing high rubber boots with the pant legs tucked inside.

And in keeping with the same theme, 400 hygiene experts gathered in Hong Kong for four days last year to discuss "The Culture of the Toilet." Said Sachiko Azai of the Japan Toilet Association, "We have to teach people how important public toilets are. We have to make toilets something we can love." Well, when it comes to loving toilets, we here in Canada take pride in the thousands and thousands of university students who hug the porcelain bowl almost every weekend.

And Sachiko, if you do have success in teaching the importance of public toilets, could you put on a seminar for architects who design Canadian shopping malls? You'd be saving kidneys, if not actual lives.

When a woman at Memorial University in St. John's was facing nudity charges after being discovered naked with a man in the library study room, school spokesman Peter Morris said, "I'll be frank: it does have its humorous elements, doesn't it?" Actually, Peter, those elements would be a lot more humorous if it was two defensive linemen from the football team caught naked in the study, and they asked you to be Frank.

Added Morris, "We have no desire for people to be nude in the library." No, but it would sure get those freshmen cracking the books earlier than ever before.

Esa Tikkanen, now of the St. Louis Blues, showed he could be as smooth off the ice as on. After meeting Gerald Ford at a charity golf tournament in Palm Springs, he asked the former president what new cars his company was coming out with this year.

My favourite quote recently came from Albert Kraus of Chicago while he attended the — I'm absolutely not making this up — Living in Leather IX convention in Toronto with 450 other aficionados of sadomasochism. Said Kraus, "Sadomasochism is practised with the heart and the mind." Good grief. What ever happened to sticks and stones?

Added Kraus, "Today we are practising safe sadomasochism." Safe sadomasochism? Believe me, I'm no expert in the field, but if you do it right, isn't somebody *supposed* to get hurt?

But the three guys I most want to have beer with are Americans Joseph VanWart, Robert White, and Johnny O'Brien.

Last year while travelling west out of New York, these three young men stopped and picked up a dog, later identified as Buddy. Buddy was digging through the trash beside a highway near Central Islip, New York, and to keep the dog from being hit, the guys loaded him into their car.

Pleased with their new friendship, the four of them proceeded to travel through New Jersey, Pennsylvania, Maryland, West Virginia, Kentucky, Missouri, Kansas, and finally to their home town of Fort Collins, Colorado. I can just imagine the fun — wolfing down burgers, all cuddled up and snoring in the back seat, taking a leak beside the road — all the things guys like to do on a long trip.

And then came the words that make guys everywhere proud. "That's when we discovered," said one of the young men from Fort Collins, who wished to remain anonymous, "that Buddy had tags." That's right, Buddy was carrying identification, which showed he hails from Central Islip, New York, not too far from that heap of garbage he was rooting through.

Look, nobody said we were the smarter of the sexes, but there's never been any doubt as to who has more fun.

To these three heroes (at least in the eyes of a smelly mutt who loves to go for long car rides), I say this, "I love you, man! But no way, Johnny, you can't have Buddy."

Buddy, by the way, has since been returned to Central Islip, New York, safe, albeit somewhat confused. He no longer accepts rides from strangers, but he's not exactly sure why.

And on that note, let's all pitch in to make 1996 The Year of the Guy.

Come on, let's hear it, everybody, now — No Wang, Boris with the pike head nose, Lash LaKraus, the Buddy wranglers — everybody repeat after me: "We have the right to remain stupid. We have the right to a rubber chicken and a whoopie cushion. If we can't afford them, the court must provide them for us."

Ye Olde Offenders Act: It's Payback Time

$\int$ OME WEEKS AGO IN TORONTO, WHERE SNEEZE GUARDS AT SALAD BARS ARE being replaced with bullet-proof glass, they had a seventeen-year-old kid running around shooting people. Not any particular people, just people older than him, because anybody his age or younger was in school. He shot four people before the cops could collar him.

Police believe they may have caught him sooner, but they were forbidden to enlist the help of the public. Why?

The Young Offenders Act. They could not release the photo or name of this potential killer because he is protected by law, by age.

Yes, there are still those in our society, walking upright and using manual dexterity, who believe that the availability of guns and protecting the young criminals who use them from prosecution are pretty good ideas. So I say we have no choice. I say we go the other way. So today, I'm introducing Ye Olde Offenders Act.

Think about it: most of us are rushing towards senior citizenship so fast we barely have time to stop and pull up our support hose. Soon there will be millions more of us than them. Fair is fair — why shouldn't the old get the same break as the young?

Ye Olde Offenders Act reads, and I quote: "Anybody over the age of fifty-five in the country of Canada will henceforth be able to do any damn fool thing he or she feels like doing — Na, na, na . . . na, na!"

Feel like taking a leak in a public fountain? Go ahead, let 'er rip. Nothing anybody can do about it.

Old man whizzing in the town fountain: "Look at this, officer — I'm the Golden Jet!"

Officer: "Are you doing what I think you're doing?"

Same man, dumping a large box of Tide into the water: "Yeah, but

look, officer — now I'm cleaning it up! Ha, ha, ha."

Officer: "Come over here. How old are you?"

Man: "Well, I'm over fifty-five!"

Officer: "According to Ye Olde Offenders Act, Section 24, Subsection 34, you're old enough not to know better. Hold out your wrists." Slap! "Okay, you can go."

Ye Olde Offenders Act — you're gonna love it.

You want to check forty items through the eight-items-or less counter? Be my guest. What are they going to do? Call a cop? They call a cop and you can tell him to go jump in the fountain.

You see, the Young Offenders Act assumes anybody under the age of eighteen committing a crime is not a criminal. He's a social problem. He's actually the bad fruit of the loins of people who thought partying and parenting were somehow related. So according to our justice system (motto: Leniency for All!) these kiddy killers are social problems.

Well, when my Ye Olde Offenders Act kicks in, the government is going to have a bunch more social problems on its hands and these non-criminals are not going to be a lot of fun to deal with because their prostates and plumbing are always acting up. Think about it: We'll never have to worry about the government de-indexing our pensions. Short of cash? We'll just get a bunch of boys from the bowling team and we'll rob a bloody bank! (Please note: if you're going to rob banks with other senior citizens, bring along a young person who can remember where the getaway car is parked. Later you can pin the crime on him. He's young! He's got the time to do the time.)

No, you won't have to worry about juvenile delinquents by the year 2000. It'll be the senile delinquents you'll walk across the street to avoid. We be bad. And if we weren't shrinking so much, we'd be in your face.

We'll do the damnedest things ever heard of and walk away whistling because we are not criminals. No, we are social problems high on bran and racing on roughage. We're not responsible for our behaviour, it's our kids' fault.

Plus, we won't cost as much to control. If they start jailing young offenders, they're going to have to build more juvenile institutions. But not for old offenders. We already have our penal institutions — they're called nursing homes.

And the best is, we can use Ye Olde Offenders Act to override the Young Offenders Act. When a whole bunch of us old people see a couple of kids committing a crime, we'll just grab the little buggers and whale the bejeesus out of them.

There'll be more of us and — that's right — of course we can't be charged. We're too old!

It'll be great. We'll call ourselves The Hole in the Wall of the·Heart Gang. No! How about Grumpy Old Gunmen? No! The Bad Bran Bunch. Yeah, that's it. And I'll be Wiley Ol' Willy. No! I'll be the Prostate Punk and you can be Lizzie 2% Borden.

I'm warning you young delinquents out there — if we can manage to stay awake long enough, we'll be your worst nightmare!

I'm Way Too Young to Be a Curmudgeon

RECENTLY I HAD A BIRTHDAY AND I'D LIKE TO TAKE A MOMENT TO THANK those readers who took the time to send me a note or a card, all expressing some very sincere cheap shots.

The "I respect you, as I do all my elders" from the retired teacher was not the lowest blow I took, but the only one printable here.

Doesn't anybody buy nice birthday cards any more? At what point did birthday-card creators decide that they should convey a message sure to make you feel lower than the flat tire on a truck in a country and western song? It's like somewhere along the line Hallmark was a victim of a hostile takeover by the Don Rickles Corporation. And they're very expensive, as insults go.

I had a lousy birthday, thank you. I received a cake with forty-eight smouldering twigs on top, mainly because my mother had a birthday only a few weeks before mine, depleting the world supply of wax. (Please, when it comes to delivering the cheap shots, leave it to a licensed professional.)

I never thought of myself as old until Thanksgiving Monday, when I was sitting on my breakwall at sunset having a drink with a friend when she said, innocently enough, "It's going to be chilly tonight." To which I said, enthusiastically, "Yeah, it'll be a good night for sleeping."

Then I quickly jerked my head around to see who the dork was that said that.

A good night for sleeping? Old people say things like that. People named Sully and Myrtle say things like that. These are people who overuse the word *my*, as in "I gotta have *my* morning coffee" and "I gotta get *my* eight hours."

It wasn't that long ago that a good night for me was when I got home too late to do any sleeping. Now here I am at sunset, looking forward to eight or nine hours of unconsciousness, like it might be a lot of fun.

I must admit, I kind of redeemed myself a few hours later and pulled myself out of the funk. This actually happened. I had smoked a turkey all day, but when guests arrived around eight, the butterball still wasn't done. So the cocktail hour stretched to two and I was out by the shed, feeding hickory sticks to the smoker, when the wife of a friend of mine came by and asked, "Do you mind if I take a peek at the bird?"

"As long as you don't tell your husband," I said and I felt so wonderfully young and immature again. Hey, you can find new friends anywhere, even the bus station. But how often do you get a chance to relive a moment of ill-spent youth?

By definition, I believe I'm much too young to be a curmudgeon. To be a curmudgeon, you have to impersonate Andy Rooney, growling and jowling at anybody under fifty and everything that makes you irregular.

By rights, I believe I'm getting too old to be a smart-ass. Taking flying leaps at rolling doughnuts is a job for somebody who doesn't have to ice his lower back every time he jogs.

As you might have guessed, I've reached an attitude plateau in my life, a crossroads of the currents of age. And I'm very frustrated, like a centipede with athlete's foot, a beaver with gingivitis, Captain Hook with hemorrhoids. There was a time when I believed I'd take my life before I started a nostalgic whine with "Why, when I was your age . . ."

But here goes.

Do you think kids today know the basic theory behind the baseball cap? Do they realize the guy who invented this most practical head shield meant for the peak to be worn in the front to keep the sun out of your eyes and the bird droppings off your nose?

Is it possible I'm missing a fashion statement here with kids wearing ball hats backwards? Like raindrops keep falling on my face and that's the way I like it, uh-huh, uh-huh? Like, I'd rather be a Rudolph than a redneck? Like, from a distance it looks like I'm headed your way, but really we're just drifting farther apart each day?

Do you think kids realize that by wearing their ball hats backwards and forcing that clump of hair through the back vent hole, they are infringing on U.S. Patent #1506739, namely the mad cowlick?

Do you think today's kids are wearing their clothes baggy just to conceal gross and unsightly things, namely other kids?

Do kids realize they're messing with the natural order or things when they wear clothes so bright rainbows are shrieking with envy?

Do you think kids walking towards you, four abreast, know I have no choice but to bust through the line off centre or rush to the outside and submarine the tight end?

Do you think kids know they run a health risk when they pass a thin, hand-rolled cigarette around the circle, trying to hold the smoke in until they nearly choke? Why, when I was a kid, we had our own packs of weeds and they had filters on them too.

I must be losing it. Somebody mentions the word *hip* and the first thing that comes to my mind is replacement.

I wouldn't say my advancing age has suddenly changed my perspective on kids, but I'm not even speaking to my secretary's boys. For years, they came to me with questions on history, which I answered eagerly, assuming Karen had told them I'd majored in the subject. Now I find out they knew the answers all along — they just wanted to hear from an eyewitness.

This generation imbalance I seem to be suffering from may have been the reason I became a rock 'n' roll roadie this past summer. REO Speedwagon, Pat Benatar, KC and the Sunshine Band, Fleetwood Mac, the Beach Boys, the Village People, the Gypsy Kings, and Jimmy Buffett — yes, folks, it's safe to say I went to more rock concerts last summer than a Deadhead with a credit card.

I attended two concerts at Molson Park at Ontario Place in Toronto, and after spending a lot of time with the young and smiling security staff there, I would like to take this public opportunity to request each and every one of you be fired. You people couldn't organize a pie-eating contest in Betty Crocker's kitchen. Pointless line-ups, repeated security checks, routing us first this way, then the other, closing off five perfectly good entrances to the grass area and herding us all through the one at the far end. You know, if you make us walk too much, muscle tissue will form and we won't be worth a damn at the stockyard auction.

You should see the look on the faces of Americans after you tell them yes, this is Molson Park and no, you cannot have a beer while you watch the show.

What's next? Are you going to start telling the bands to turn their music down?

But hey, did I have a great time? Wonderful. And why? Because I'm a baby boomer shoutin' and stompin' to save rock 'n' roll music from the evil and immoral forces within our society known as "today's music."

Okay, so I made a little mistake. It turns out the Gypsy Kings are not even remotely related to Romanian royalty. But at least they don't call themselves Meat Puppets, Urge Overkill, Jesus Lizard (I'm not making even one of these names up), Hootie and the Blowfish, or Toad the Wet Sprocket. (Actually, I kind of like that last one: "Ladies and gentlemen, let's hear it for Sonny Bono and Toad the Wet Sprocket!")

I love Jimmy Buffett, but I am most definitely not a Parrothead. I did, however, enjoy the fat guy who was wearing a crown of fresh-picked carrots bumping into everybody, saying, "I could have sworn they said something about Carrotheads." He was obviously misinformed.

The Village People were great. Representing male American machoism, they still take to the stage dressed as a construction worker, a U.S. Marine, a cowboy, an Indian, a biker, and a cop. I got a little queasy when the biker kept saying to the cop, "Frisk me, big guy!" But that's show biz.

Fortunately, the Village People have remained in their '70s characters. If they updated to the '90s, they'd have to dress up as a disgraced elected official, a pro athlete chained to a briefcase, a computer hacker, a street person, a disgruntled postal worker, and Tony Robbins.

Mick Fleetwood put on a concert at the ball park in Buffalo with his band of six people he picked up hitchhiking on the way into town. By the time he was done introducing all the new members of Fleetwood Mac, his time was up.

So why do boomers like me attend rock concerts where we shake (it's mostly in the right hand, Doc), rattle (if I ice after I play, the noise goes away), and rock 'n' roll?

Simply put, we proudly congregate by the thousands and act like we're all having the same seizure because we are making a unified generation statement. We are saying we don't mosh and we don't wear Doc Martens. We are rock 'n' rollers, for godsakes. When we pass a person over our heads at a concert, it's to prevent that person from puking on our desert boots.

We are collectively denying we had anything to do with the creation of bell-bottoms, the sitar, or Barry Manilow. We are telling the younger generations that we know what Billy Joe McAllister threw off the Talahatchee Bridge — and you couldn't beat it out of us if you tried.

We are looking to the Heavens and we are asking the King to give us a sign, a clue, a revelation on how it is possible that Keith Richards is still alive.

We are saying, our music of the '60s and '70s is the best music ever written from this point in time back to biblical days when Sodom and the Salt Licks released *Don't Look Back*.

We are saying you can body-slam and in-line skate your alternative, cyber-pop, underground punk pit, skid-marked music by Shanking Pickle and Swinging Udders until the cows come home and you will never, I repeat never, have fun, fun, fun 'til Daddy takes your T-Bird away. Oh, yeah.

No, I'm sorry, we are the boomers and we cornered the market on music and it's all in the words — the intelligence, the grace, the sheer weight of the words that tell you who we are.

You can head-bang yourselves into the millennium before you ever come up with:

Went to a dance
Lookin' for romance
Saw Barbara Ann
And I thought I'd take a chance
On Barbara Ann . . . Ba, Ba, Ba, Ba . . . Barbara Ann (repeat 57 times)
Tried Betty Sue
Tried Betty Lou
Tried Mary Lou
(At this point, I almost tried Lou! Yikes!)
But I knew it wouldn't do
Oh, Barbara Ann . . . Oh, Barbara Ann . . .

(repeat Ba . . . Ba . . . line until Cher's next bum tuck)

A Guy's Guide to Good Housekeeping

IN THE PAST YEAR I'VE HAD SO MANY CLEANING LADIES COME AND GO AT MY house, they've set up a "Take a Number" system at the kitchen door. I can't understand it. I'm not a real stickler for neatness. A little dusting, a little vacuuming, scrub and polish a few floors, take my clothes home and bring them back clean, replace the odd shingle on the roof, cut the lawn, paint the shed — where else are you going to make twenty bucks that easy?

Knowing what I know about house cleaning, if I were setting up house to live alone (solitary confinement with unlimited day and night passes), there are a few general rules I'd follow faithfully.

First and foremost, buy all your fabric furniture, pillows, and rugs in the same colour. Make sure that colour perfectly matches the colour of your cat's fur. You can save yourself years of vacuuming and eventually, if left to thicken and mesh, the furry fabrics will take on an expensive angora look.

Have an artistic friend come in and paint landscapes on all your windows. That way, when the dirt and grime builds up on the glass, it just looks like the nearby countryside is dirty.

Beat the buildup of dishes in the sink — keep only one table setting of everything. That way, when all your cutlery and all your china have been used, it still looks like you've just had a light snack. Paper and plastic are fine for guests. After all, when you're single, the object is to get invited out to dinner, not play host to the masses.

For single people, the refrigerator becomes the chilling museum. A few simple rules apply. If it's green and showing vital signs of life, but not in the vegetable crisper, toss it. Anything in the freezer wrapped in a newspaper headlined "Trudeau to Divorce" ought to be carefully examined before consumption. When fruit shrivels up to the point where you can't tell your oranges from your McIntosh apples, throw them into a high-speed blender, add white rum, and call them daiquiris. And if all your cheeses look like blue cheese, but you don't buy blue cheese, you might consider making a deposit at your nearest bacteria research bank.

Pet control is important to singles because when there's only two of you, who wants to be in second place? You can easily keep the cat from sleeping at the foot of the bed by spraying that area with heavy doses of WD-40. After he slips off a few times in his sleep, he'll find an alternative spot at ground level. To combat those tell-tale cat odours, I regularly add a little Old Spice cologne to his drinking water, and I crush one or two breath mints into his Seafood Supreme.

Dust balls, if lacquered and threaded with string, can make inexpensive and interesting ornaments at holiday time. Small rugs and mats can be easily and quickly cleaned by hanging them on your car aerial before you drive through the car wash. And remember, those gobs of toothpaste that cling to the sink make fine after-dinner mints when dried.

Sometimes a change is as good as real house cleaning. For instance, if you don't have time to do thorough room-to-room purgation of the place, I find that merely moving the pizza boxes and the empty bottles from one room to another can give you a fresh outlook on things.

Occasionally things will get beyond your control. You're in trouble when the cat prefers living in the toolshed, or your friends ask you to meet them at the corner for drinks when the party's supposed to be at your place.

At the point when the painted landscapes look like summer in Sudbury and vultures are gathering on your windowsills, you have three options: seal off certain rooms with "Time Capsule" signs, sandblast your house from the inside, or host a family dinner.

The family dinner option is the most fun and the least expensive. Haul out the plastic forks, the paper plates, and the green cheese fondue and invite your loved ones over. No self-respecting siblings can stand idly by and watch you being slowly soiled to death in your own house. By the time you and the brother-in-law have figured out what's wrong with the Blue Jays over beer and pretzels, the house looks like the centrefold in *Better Homes and Gardens*. Presto! Safe for another six months.

And really, isn't that what families are for? Keeping the single male members from having to appear before a board of health?

Driving: Something Else You Can Do with a Car

IN TODAY'S GADGET-MAD SOCIETY, THE TREADMILL-TO-TOYS RAT RACE IN which the rats appear to be in (remote) control, many rites of passage are falling through the cracks of technology. For instance, when exactly did the dashboard of the car become a desktop data-processing centre?

One thing for sure, the ol' father-and-son family car ritual sure ain't what it used to be.

"Okay, Jimmy, here's the key, son. Now . . . No, no, Jimmy, don't put that key in the ignition. This key, Jimmy, is for the cellular phone centre. It unlocks the 832-channel spectrum and the 32-digit automatic dialling deck.

"You see, Jimmy, you can lock your car and somebody can still steal it, but without this key, son, nobody can ever break the electronic code of your personalized instant international I.D. profile.

"Okay, son, now turn the ignition . . . That's it, and just head down the highway while I explain the operation of today's high-tech automobile.

"Now, Jimmy, pay close attention to those indicators. What? Oh, no, son, we don't worry about gas or oil lights. You run out, you just pick up the phone and CAA will come and get you. If they don't get to you in thirty minutes, I think you get a free pizza or something.

"Anyway, press this button right here. What? The windshield washer? Ha, what a kid. No, this is your speaker mute for private calls . . . know what I mean, Jimmy?

"And this button is for Call-in-Progress override, so if the car stalls at high speed in heavy traffic, your phone conversation won't get cut off.

"Well, sure, I suppose you could hit the emergency flasher when that happens, but remember, Jimmy, if the customer gets cut off just as he's about to give you his purchase order number, those flashers aren't going to bring back your fat commission cheque, now, are they, son?

"What's that? Oh, that beeping. No, that's not the seatbelt alarm. Boy, where do kids come up with these ideas? No, Jimmy, that beep means Call Waiting.

"Actually, I ripped out the seatbelts the day I bought the car. Their alarm mechanism was causing static on the CD player.

"Well sure they say that seatbelts save lives, but if you're all buckled up, Jimmy, just how are you going to reach over here and work this little baby? It's the latest in laptops, Jimmy. Built-in disc drive, and watch this . . . POP! . . . up comes the screen. Look at that — this week's fantasy baseball scores.

Dammit, Jimmy, you gotta be more careful. When you skidded around the last turn, your brake foot kicked out the plug on the battery pack and now the computer is down.

"Remember, Jimmy, good driving requires great concentration. What? A flashing red light? Might be just a traffic light with a short circuit, son, just cruise through it . . .

"Geez, I think we lost the seating plan for your sister's wedding off the computer screen . . .

"What? We just clashed side mirrors with a transport truck? Did I mention solid double lines mean don't pass, Jimmy? No? Well, they do.

"Here, Jimmy, just yell 'home' into this box. No, I mean it. Yell 'home.'

"Hi, honey . . . Ain't that something . . . Yeah, Jimmy's doing great. He's just activated the E-Z Dial 11 VocalLink to call you on the cellular . . . Yeah, 'Look, Ma, no hands!' Ha, ha, ha, what a kid!

"Jimmy, put your hands down, now! I was just joking with your mother.

"Look, honey, fax me the seating plan for Jeannette's wedding. I want to stop at the caterer's.

"What's that, son? No. Generally speaking, there's not enough room between a tandem trailer and the guardrail. Better pass him on the left.

"Yeah, honey, it's coming through now. Thanks. What do you think, Jimmy? Crystal clear, eh? Portafax! Cellular-compatible, international range. Amazing, eh?

"Why, just last week Henderson faxed me a revised agenda for the national sales meeting from his seat on an Air Canada flight over Winnipeg. Can you believe it? Sending fax messages to earth from an airplane. Problem was, I have no idea who Henderson is. Must have misdialled. But from an airplane to a car . . . incredible!

"*Look out!* Geez, Jimmy! Well, I didn't think it was necessary to explain the difference between the on and off ramp, son. I mean, it's pretty obvious.

"You better get serious, Jimmy, driving can be a dangerous —

"What? Yes, it does matter which way you go on a one-way street.

"As I was saying, Jimmy, you remember when Herb Mathewson drove off the Skyway and they had to wait until spring to get him and his car out of the bottom of the bay?

"Well, yes, it was windy on the Skyway, but the fact is, Herb was having a fight with his wife on the cellular and playing a little Nintendo on the laptop when his boss faxes him his dismissal papers. Herb lost it, Jimmy. He pressed all the wrong buttons and the battery pack exploded, driving the internal scanner aerial up his nose. The coroner said the E-Z VocalLink hit Herb so hard on the side of the head, he could read the toll-free service number on his right temple. They had to bury poor Herb with the acoustic coupler still around his neck.

"Oil light? No, no . . . that's the recording light on my answering machine. You see, sometimes if I'm working at the computer and faxing back reports to the office, I'll put the answering machine on. I get a big laugh when people call me in the car and my message says, 'I'm not in right now!' Get it?

"Oh no, Jimmy, not a chance, son. Turn that off. If you're going to operate a motor vehicle properly, you're most certainly not going to listen to rock music on the radio.

"Good driving, Jimmy, requires great concentration. What? Sure. If you have a free hand, use it to steer."

She-Drivers

*S*HE *MAGAZINE*, A BRITISH PUBLICATION, RECENTLY REVEALED THE RESULTS OF a reader survey in which almost 90 percent of women drivers say they are as competent at driving as men, but nearly two-thirds say their partner thinks he is a better driver and constantly criticizes their performance.

Of course men criticize women drivers. I openly criticize women drivers on the highway with such a wide variety of hand gestures, I usually wind up steering the damn car with my knees. Women drive me nuts on the road.

First they signal, then they turn. When they come up to a stop sign, they slow down, brake, and come to a stop. On the highway, they drive the speed limit, for godsakes. Believe me, when a guy's gotta get somewhere, the last thing he needs between him and his destination are people who obey the rules of the road. Namely, She-Drivers.

Constantly criticize their performance? Are you kidding?

What guys desperately want is for every car to be equipped with a phone and a bumper sticker listing the car's phone number. That way, when we get behind women drivers on the highway, we won't have to tailgate them and flash our lights on and off. That way, we can just call them up and tell them to get the hell out of the way. American tourists who drive 55 mph in the passing lane on our major highways would be issued a toll-free 1-800 number.

We also want the right to mount emergency flashers and sirens on our cars so we can scare old people right out of the fast lane. Real guys would like to see bumping from behind legalized and side-swiping reduced to a misdemeanour.

You see, women don't understand men, and nothing underscores this more dramatically than driving a car. For better or for worse, we men (and I think I speak for every guy out there who believes every woman he has to pass on the highway is a moron and every woman who passes him is an idiot) are descendants of explorers and adventurers. Despite hundreds and hundreds of years of ingesting large amounts of tobacco, alcohol, and pork rinds, we have not been able to rid ourselves of this nomadic pioneer spirit.

Face it: there are no more oceans to navigate, there are no more far-off lands to settle, and we're two years away from seeing a Planet Hollywood Restaurant atop Mount Everest. The highway is our last frontier, the automobile is our conquering chariot, and women drivers are in our way.

Our daily quest to conquer the unknown and set a land speed record in doing so dates back to our heroes of history like Christopher Columbus, who in searching for a passage to India discovered America instead. We're damn proud of that man. Sure, he missed his target by half the earth's circumference and a lot of his passengers died along the way, but not once did he stop and ask for directions. And for his era, he made excellent time.

Ladies, you just don't understand. I mean, if guys could refuel their cars while moving at high speed, like military planes on long-range bombing missions, don't you think we would?

Why do guys illegally drive across train tracks? Because the flashing lights, the dangling bells, and the gates across the road represent a challenge. Sure, the train is bigger and faster, but the car is more mobile, not being connected to tracks and such.

A yield sign? Ha! Another of our heroes, Winston Churchill, spoke for all guys when he said: "We will drive on the beaches, we shall drive on the fields and in the streets. We shall drive in the hills and in the malls — and we shall never, ever surrender."

Once, while driving to Florida, my brother-in-law Danny spotted a construction sign that warned "Speed Limit 50 Ahead." Danny figured out there were, like, two of us, eh? So we could go 100. And we did, because we're guys, dammit.

The survey results in *She Magazine* also found women are twice as likely as men to stay sober and drive home after a party. What are women saying here? Are they saying that they'd rather stay sober and drive home themselves than ride in the same car with the guy behind the wheel who, on the way there, made two moves that the safety censors stripped out of *Cannonball Run* and now that he's had a couple drinks, he's feeling kind of daring? Is that it?

But what drives men nuts about women drivers is how they can drive defensively, how they don't try to run slow drivers off the road, and how they never try to cut into a lane of traffic with a car where there's barely enough room for a motorcycle. This makes guys particularly crazy because — we taught them how to drive! Go figure, eh?

PART II

Globe-Trotting Guys

A Postie Goes to Portugal

D ID I MENTION THAT DANNY PATAKFALVI IS A CONSCIENTIOUS POSTAL worker, a great guy, and my brother-in-law, technically speaking? Well, he is.

I was once married to Danny's sister, a relationship that unfortunately ended with a "she got the car, I got the cat" deal after six good years. And one more, making it a total of seven.

The car has long since been sold for parts, the cat died a couple of years ago, but I'll be damned if I can get rid of Danny. This kid couldn't take a hint if it came in pill form with a glass of water on the side.

So I went to Europe and Danny tagged along and it was great. It really was. *Beauty*-ful was the way Danny described it. As you might imagine, Europe was a real eye-opener for Danny, a postie in Welland, Ontario, who regularly gets lost on the route he's had since 1984.

I made one serious strategic error in travelling with my brother-in-law in that, after I agreed to go, I . . . okay, make that two serious strategic errors.

After I agreed to go, I put Danny in charge of the driving. In my position of official navigator, translator, and sightseeing guide, I was deeply disappointed in not being able to use my talents, because as the official driver, Danny did not stop, except to sleep, and even then, sometimes at the wheel. After landing in Lisbon from Toronto, we drove south to Alentejo, north to Garda, east to Spain through Malaga, then southeast to Africa and Morocco, then we stopped because Danny felt that was enough for the first day.

Early on in the trip, there were several disagreements about the daily itinerary, but Danny stuck to his claim that during all the preparation sessions, no mention was ever made of stopping.

Roaring north out of Lisbon, we passed through the picturesque mountain village of Belem, where I pointed out for Danny the famed

tomb of Portugal's greatest explorer, Vasco da Gama, who sailed from here in 1497 and returned in triumph having discovered the passage to India. Without even slowing down, Danny said, "India?" and asked me to pass him the map.

Don't get the wrong impression of Danny. It's not that he didn't appreciate such cultural landmarks, because as we were leaving Belem, I pointed out the five-storey Monument to the Discoveries, and without even taking his eyes off the road he shouted enthusiastically: "*Beauty*-ful."

And I must admit we were running late, because just north of this lush and ancient village on the banks of the meandering, azure River Tagus, Danny had to "brush back some *mulliac* on a moped" who made the mistake of thinking his licence plate gave him some kind of right to be on the same road as us. We'd lost valuable time, but Danny felt the guy learned his lesson and wouldn't try that again.

We went to Seville, the heartbeat of Spain, with its mysterious winding alleys, secluded, sun-drenched patios, and jasmine-scented gardens. At least that's what the guidebook claimed. I didn't actually see any of this because we went to and through Seville, as Danny likes to say, "like ripe grain through a loose goose!" We did Seville in less than thirty minutes, and, if it wasn't for "a bunch of noon-hour geeks and gawkers," Danny feels we could have done much better. All I saw was a man with an overturned bread cart in the rearview mirror, shaking his fist at us near the Cathedral de Seville.

I couldn't tell if Danny was referring to the upset bread seller or the great Gothic stained-glass windows surrounding the 184-foot-high Moorish minaret, but I remember him saying with a lot of gusto: "*Beauty*-ful!"

All told, we passed by, but did not visit, the tomb of Vasco da Gama in Belem, the mausoleum of Henry the Navigator in Sagres, and even the shrine to Christopher Columbus in Seville, because as Danny said (and he does have a point here), these were all just dead guys who couldn't pump gas or give directions.

So for Danny, Europe was strictly a matter of speed and mileage. For me — not that I mind sitting in a car for fourteen or fifteen long, hot, sweaty hours at a time — it was a little tiring.

I shouldn't say we never stopped. In Tangiers, Danny purchased a leather bag, and he had nothing but positive things to say about the efficiency of a marketing system that allows you to shop through your driver's window. Near Badajoz, Spain, he stopped and had me take a photo of him beside an old man on a donkey so he could tell all the guys back at the post office he'd met Juan Valdez on his holidays. And in the town of Meda, he stopped and introduced himself to a fellow of letters, a comrade in envelopes, a uniformed, helmeted Portuguese postie on a motor scooter.

The man was polite, even though his helmet appeared to bring an enormous amount of pressure on his ears and forehead. But he had little time for us. He explained to me that in Europe posties have to push through their routes quickly so they can be finished and in the *taverna* by no later than one o'clock in the afternoon. When I translated this to Danny, he said: "*Beauty*-ful!"

Our European motor tour became our ultimate bonding experience in the sense that we spent so much time driving on oppressively hot days, a few times we actually stuck together.

But we did a lot of European-type things too. For instance, after evening meals I explained to Danny the quaint continental custom of "taking the air." Danny enjoyed this, and we did it a lot. It's just that he preferred to call it "bar-hoppin'."

And I think Danny learned a lot on his first trip abroad. Like you can't wash your hands with chicken and noodles even though the words *sopa* and *soup* have a similar sound to them. Danny learned the hard way that if a toilet doesn't have a toilet seat, it's probably not a toilet. He also learned that a herd of goats in the road has the right of way unless you want your licence plate butted clean off.

Danny really took to the language, though he had trouble with the money. In Portugal, he kept referring to the currency of escudos (pronounced ess-ku-dosh) as "mosquitoes" and more than once he got short-changed when he put down travellers' cheques and got back insect repellent. In Spain, Danny referred to pesetas (puh-say-tas) as "pesto," so we enjoyed some nice, unordered rice dishes as well.

But the highlight of Danny's adventures in foreign languages occurred in the Spanish town of Moron (honest!), where he went into a bank to change a small amount of "mosquitoes" for the equivalent in "pestos." After he completely baffled two bank tellers, he put the cash away and pulled out his travellers' cheques. Waving the cheques and repeating the word "cheque" quite loudly out of frustration caused the manager to come out of his office "to help solve this customer's problem" (or, as a Spaniard explained to me later, "to lose the foreign geek").

The manager was very patient, and after hearing Danny repeat the word another dozen times, gently led him down the street to a place where they sell chicken. I'm not making this up.

And did the kid get discouraged? On the contrary, Danny returned to the car with the good news that a whole chicken done on the spit in Spain only costs about 8,000 mosquitoes.

On the way out of town, Danny and I had our picture taken beside the town's sign after we took a magic marker and put an s on Moron.

Danny has that insightful curiosity critical to a traveller of the world. For instance, after leaving Moron, we were cruising down a four-lane Spanish autopista when Danny said, "Ah, Bill, this autopista thing — does that mean everybody on this highway is drunk?" Is it any wonder I love this guy?

And isn't that the real beauty of travelling to Europe — to open the mind, experience another culture, be exposed to new ideas?

We had such a great time, we're going again as soon as we can save enough money for the air fare. As Danny says, "Save those mosquitoes and we'll be on the big bird before you know it!"

I hope this account of my travels with Danny doesn't give you the wrong impression. I had a terrific time. I really did. In only three weeks, I got to see every town in Portugal, Spain, the northern part of Africa, and I think once, while I was asleep in the back seat, we went through France and Germany.

And when I got home, part of me was the picture of good health. My body was white as a ghost, of course, but my right arm, the one I had hanging out the passenger window, looked like it could have belonged to Oscar Peterson.

No, really, it was great. In fact, I wished I had Danny with me the first time I went to Europe for a year, back in the '70s. I could have done the whole damn thing in less than a month.

The Simpson Saga as Told by My Housesitter

A FEW DAYS BEFORE RETURNING HOME TO CANADA, I FOUND MYSELF SITTING on the proverbial sun-drenched patio in Portugal (to be honest, though, there were some axiomatic clouds closing in from the west) and the waiter approached the table with a phone. My call home to check on my cat had finally been put through.

From the moment my housesitter said hello, I knew something was wrong.

"Is Weggie okay?" I asked.

"Yeah, Weggie's fine," she said, breathlessly. "But it looks like O. J. Simpson may have murdered his wife." O. J. Simpson? Murder? His wife?

Suddenly, I, too, was talking in panicked, hushed tones.

"Well, is O.J. headed north to Wainfleet, for godsakes? Did he leave some kind of note? Did he mention Weggie by name?" I asked. I know this cat can irritate just about anyone, but . . . O. J. Simpson? "Is this guy totally out of control or what?" I asked.

"Actually, he's in a white Bronco on the San Diego Freeway," she said. "I'm watching the chase on TV."

"You're watching the chase on TV?" I repeated.

"Yeah," she said. "They're televising the chase live on all major networks."

I thought for a moment. "You know that one key I left you? The one I said you should never use? The one that opens the liquor cabinet?" I asked. "You didn't use that key, did you?"

"No, no. They're chasing O.J. all over the L.A. freeways. It's been on for about half an hour."

"The chase has lasted half an hour?" I asked.

"Yeah," she said. "But they're only going forty miles an hour."

I thought to myself, of course the chase could only go at forty miles an hour. How else could the colour commentators have time to do their voice-over?

I was still confused, but I decided to take a shot. "Do you think O.J. knows that if he went faster, it would be a better chase and he'd actually have a greater chance of escaping?"

"Actually," she said, "O.J.'s in the back seat with a gun."

That's not so unusual. I've driven on the freeways in L.A. And the fact he's steering and working the pedals from the back seat — well, that explains why the best he can do is forty miles an hour. Now it was starting to make sense.

"There must be like twenty cop cars chasing him," she said.

I was paying for this call, so I took another shot. "From what you know so far, do you think the cops realize if they went faster it would be a better chase and they'd have a greater chance of catching him?"

"There must be twenty helicopters chasing him, too," she said.

"The cops are chasing him with helicopters?" I asked.

"No, I told you. The cops are chasing him in cars. The reporters are chasing him in helicopters," she said.

"At any time, have they cut away to Steven Spielberg sitting in a director's chair with a megaphone?" I asked.

"No, but there's people on the overpasses and they're waving and cheering," she said.

"Are you sure it's not just an ad for Hertz?" I asked. "Like a new preferred customer protection plan or something?"

"I don't think so," she said. "One commentator said O.J. might shoot himself right there in the back seat."

Hey, I write for television. He kills himself, that's the end of the chase scene right there.

"Listen, how's Weggie?" I asked. And that's went the line went dead.

Great! It just cost me fifty bucks to phone home to listen to a housesitter, who obviously had been into my single-malt collection, describe to me a celebrity episode of *TV's Bloopers and Practical Jokes*.

I went back to the room and told Danny and he looked at me like the green wines of Portugal had finally taken their poisonous toll.

When I woke up the next morning, I thought maybe I'd dreamed the whole thing.

Two days later at the airport in Lisbon, I spotted a group of Canadians coming off the Canada 3000 plane that we were taking back. I approached a guy wearing a Blue Jays cap.

"How the Jays doing?" I asked.

"Awful!" he said. "Hey! Did you hear about O. J. Simpson?"

Lord, it was true — the chase, the cops, the live coverage, the . . .

"Uh, look," I asked in a very low voice, "this may sound kind of silly, but, uh, there wasn't a cat involved in that thing, was there?"

"Nah, I don't think so," he replied. "But there was something about a dog."

How I Got Ejected from a Cuban Cemetery

IN 1959, AFTER FIVE YEARS IN MEXICAN EXILE, FIDEL CASTRO HIT THE beaches of Cuba driven by four simple words: "Liberty, Democracy, Social Justice." (It was easier back then because Castro did not have to navigate around all the people on rafts, headed in the opposite direction.)

In 1994, after surviving Christmas with my family, I too hit the beaches of Cuba driven by four simple words: "Sell Off" and "All Inclusive."

I know, I know — many would argue that vacationing in Cuba only helps finance the fascist and fanatical dictatorship of Fidel Castro. But since travelling to Cuba really rankles the fascist and fanatical Jesse Helms, Newt Gingrich, and Rush Limbaugh, I call that a draw.

(Warning: our Foreign Affairs department in Ottawa has issued an important travel advisory to Canadian tourists entering the United States: "Caution should be taken so that you're not crushed by fat, loud, rich, white guys goose-stepping in the streets. This new phenomenon is known as the Rush Limbaugh-da.")

Meanwhile, back in Cuba, I went, I saw, I got bounced out of the cemetery in Santiago.

Cuba, as you know, is the lush and languid Caribbean island still firmly in the guerrilla grip of the bearded dictator Fidel. Fidel, according to himself, is a visionary. Fidel never tires of telling his people that he is systematically shaping Cuba to become a very different Caribbean nation. Unfortunately, that nation is Haiti.

How the Cubans — the sweetest, the most resourceful people in all the islands — maintain a sense of dignity and class amid all the misery and decay around them is astounding to a visitor.

I stayed at the Delta Sierra Mar Resort in the very south of Cuba. And it's quite compelling: you drive up to the tropical, arched entrance with the jungle-like Sierra Maestra mountains above, the turquoise Caribbean sea below, and as you enter the lobby — there they are, the heroes of Cuba depicted in huge posters on the walls: Eric Lindros, Doug Gilmour, and Felix Potvin. I'm not making this up. I know the Delta is Canadian-operated, but please — if I wanted to see posters of hockey players, I'd have stayed at the Delta Chelsea Inn in Toronto.

So to see the real Cuba, I signed up for the Santiago de Cuba city tour, which included excursions to the rum factory, the cigar factory, and the cemetery.

Many took the tour to escape the hotel policy of playing "Guantanamera" non-stop twenty-four hours a day. Of all the things Cuba needs, a new national song ought to be given top priority.

Once aboard the tour bus, Angel, our tour guide who can name more Canadian cities than our own minister of transportation, introduced us to Pedro, "the best bus driver in all of Cuba, who has never had an accident . . . yet . . . today!"

This got big laughs all around the bus.

Not far from the hotel, the bus pulled over, and Angel explained to us the military circumstances that surrounded a half-sunken Spanish galleon we could clearly see in the bay to our right. Then some wienie, who I'm ashamed to say was Canadian, asked Angel if the ship had been destroyed by cannons from the nearby fort or by airplanes. Angel, I must say, was very gentle in his response that, had military airplanes been invented by the time of the Spanish American War, the Cubans would not have hesitated to use them. (All right, it's true I did major in history at university, but frankly I wasn't all that focused from 1969 through 1972. It was early. My questions got a lot better later.)

The tour didn't get off to what would be described as a rollicking start. After a one-hour drive to the city of Santiago, the rum factory was closed due to labour problems. We were, however, allowed into the tasting room, where we sampled three-, five- and seven-year-old rums. Even the teetotallers and recovering alcoholics hit the hard stuff after forty minutes of non-stop — you guessed — "Guantanamera" by the rum-factory house band.

I'm sure if you looked hard enough, somewhere in Cuba you could find a newsstand with its own house band.

The tour didn't make a rousing recovery from its initial setback because the cigar factory was also closed due to labour problems, or staff holidays, or possibly a period of national mourning for the house band, who were summarily executed by the previous tour group for playing — everybody now — "Guantanamera."

At this point, I was getting a little disillusioned. After all the screwups, I thought if we get to the Santiago cemetery and it turns out we can't see the tomb of the great Cuban national hero Jose Marti because he's been found not to be dead after all, this is really going to ruin my vacation.

Although most of the sights on this tour couldn't be seen on this day, the trip itself wasn't uneventful. Because at 1:30 P.M. on a narrow street in a residential section of Santiago, Pedro "the best bus driver in all of Cuba" had an accident. With no more than one hundred cars in the whole country actually operating at any given time due to the absence of oil and gas, Pedro managed to hit one of them.

Subsequently, Pedro took off in chase of the driver of the car, which didn't stop and twenty of us were stranded at a souvenir shop that sold ceramic ash trays and photos of Che Guevera.

And we loved it! Why? You guessed it — no house band.

On a new bus with a new driver, we pulled up to the famous Santiago cemetery where nobody was having labour problems. You'll find this to be true of any cemetery in any country — no walkouts.

I don't know if it was the rum, the heat, or the fact that I hadn't heard "Guantanamera" in almost an hour, but I snapped.

As we passed a crypt that was kind of crooked, Angel explained that this was the resting place of the great Cuban patriot and rum maker Don Facundo Bacardi. I'm sorry, but I couldn't resist. I asked if, due to the curvature of the casket, would this be called — *a Bacardi with a twist.*

73

Angel shot me a dagger of a look. As they say in Cuba, if looks could kill, I was at least standing in the appropriate place.

I probably should've stopped there, except the seven-year-old hard stuff was kicking in as we passed the tomb of Bacardi's nephew, right beside the old man.

"So, Angel," I said, "*a double Bacardi on ice?*"

Although no one else laughed, I got quite hysterical. When I inquired about the rum maker killed in that tragic shipwreck — "*Bacardi on the rocks*" — I was asked to leave the tour and sit on the bus. Which I did.

My ejection from this famous cemetery did not, however, stop me from rolling the window down on the bus and yelling at Angel to tell the story about the other family member who was shot when caught with drugs — "*Bacardi with coke!*" Anyway, it worked out great because on a Cuban tour bus the air conditioner is so loud, you can't hear — wait for it — "Guantanamera."

Ah hell, if we as Canadians can't visit foreign cultures and make fun of their most revered citizens with stupid little bar jokes, then I say we ought to stay home. And what's more, I'm sure they'd agree.

All together, now — "Guantanamera, na na na Guantanamera, do do do Guantanamera!"

A Tuscan Villa: "Oh Great! A Pool! Anybody Got Any Water?"

JUST THE THOUGHT OF IT: ONE LAZY, DREAMY MONTH IN THE LUSH AND rugged region of Tuscany, the place Tennyson christened "the lands of palm and southern pine."

From other travellers on other trips, we'd heard the stories about the sumptuously renovated castles and farmhouses in and around the Chianti district of northern Italy, affordable if you shopped smart and stayed long. Yes, we said, let's do it — two couples, three of us writers, one a photographer, all tennis players and seasoned travellers. None of us averse to wine.

We began by collecting brochures on villas and clipping articles on Tuscany. We scoured travel books, interrogated Italian friends, drew up lists, and assigned responsibilities — all of which required a lot of time, Chianti Classico, and northern Italian cuisine.

Once we had our villa wish list, it was presented to a Toronto tour operator/villa booking agent. She was sweet, she was accommodating, she granted our every wish. (But she, as it turns out, had never actually visited the villa!)

For a total of $4,480 we rented, for the entire month of May, one large double villa with a fireplace, a washer and a dryer, a swimming pool, a tennis court, four bicycles, a barbecue, and — my own private paradise, where I planned to laze most afternoons in a lounge chair with a book in one hand and a pole in the other — two small lakes stocked with trout. For a great price of $787 per person, we secured return-trip seats on Air France, Toronto to Rome, with a no-charge two-day stopover in Paris.

The sheer exhilaration of this lifetime adventure, the delirious anticipation of well-laid plans peaked on departure day at Pearson International Airport to the point where it set off the metal detectors. (Okay, so it was the foil in the pack of my Dentyne gum, but believe me, we were excited.)

Two days in Paris went by in a blur — an expensive, somewhat tawdry, high-cholesterol blur. We flew on to Rome.

And then suddenly, there it was, the bright and busy landscape of Italy passing by the windows of our train with Rome disappearing behind us and the red, round city of Siena six hours straight ahead. There we would pick up a rented car and . . . Hey, wait a minute. Six hours on the train gets us into Siena at five, three hours after the Avis office closes on a Saturday. Not to point fingers, but somebody (Ben) had missed a big assignment.

My travel companion and I jumped train when the error was discovered at a point seventy kilometres closer to our villa than the city of Siena would be. Ben and his wife carried on to Siena to find that the Avis people are as good as their fine-printed word — CLOSED. There was no note and the HELP-LINE didn't.

At Rapolano Terme, we lugged our bags to the main road, desperately seeking any form of transportation to our villa at Castello di Modanella. Had we known then of the generosity and graciousness of the Tuscans, an extended thumb and a helpless facial expression would have gotten us to the villa in a half-hour or so. But Chach, Rapolano's only cabbie, did the winding fourteen kilometres in less than fifteen minutes for under $25.

Gabriella, the manager of the Castello di Modanella's villa properties, directed our driver to our villa, on another picturesque hilltop across the valley from this ancient castle. She informed us our friends had called and would be arriving late in the evening from Siena, still carless.

The sun was setting on a very long day — the early dash to Charles de Gaulle Airport, the flight, the train to and then from Rome, pinned down by our luggage in the back seat for the taxi ride to the villa.

As we began to unpack, I noticed we were not in a large double villa with a fireplace but a double stone cottage. Actually, it was two bedrooms separated by a kitchen with a couch. The only fireplace we had was in the brochure, which I then laid out on the kitchen counter. There I noticed a welcome gift of a bottle of local Chianti. I uncorked it, feeling very apprehensive about a lot of things, including the fact that in no time at all, three of my travelling mates would have nothing whatsoever to drink.

My initial disappointment was short-lived, because in the soft spring light of a new day, I could clearly see the villa situation was many times worse than I imagined. Depression replaced disenchantment.

The first thing I did was stroll down to the pool to test the temperature for a morning swim. Fortunately, I'm a "pinkies first" kind of guy and not a "run and take the plunge" type. There was no water in the pool. There had not been water in the pool since the previous summer.

For a vacationer, I don't think this works. A pool without water is like a pub without ale or a tennis court without a net, which was the next feature of the villa I discovered.

Oh, there was a wire between the posts with some netting hanging from it, but the holes and sagging spaces at the top left most points in hot dispute. It was the kind of net John McEnroe must have learned to play tennis on because every second call was questioned.

Before long, we discovered the washer and dryer were not part of the villa, but located in the castle near the office for these properties. As it turned out, the washer worked, the dryer was broken.

There were bicycles, but not one for each of us. There were two bikes in bad shape, one an adult's, the other a child's. All tires were flat and the air pump was broken.

And my angler's paradise, my afternoon escape to two small secluded lakes stocked with trout? Are you ready? Two murky ponds filled with carp. I am not making a word of this up.

Oh, and the barbecue was not a barbecue but an oven at the back of a nearby farm building where, by gathering rocks and borrowing the grill from the villa's gas oven, you could create an open-fire barbecue.

That is, if you had something along the lines of food to barbecue, which we did not because by Sunday, we were still carless and two miles from the nearest stores, which are closed because . . . it's Sunday.

Gabriella was sympathetic and kind enough to give us some pasta, a jar of sauce, and some vegetables from her garden. She also recommended a local farm where the couple took in guests for dinner. "Simple and quite inexpensive" is how she described it. We walked to the farm Sunday evening for dinner. It was wonderful, a revelation in Tuscan country fare. It was also $200 Cdn. I made a mental note never to eat in a restaurant Gabriella described as "elegant but pricey."

By Monday, there was a mutiny in our midst. The couple who were friends of the Toronto booking agent thought we should persevere with our situation and not make a fuss. I, on the other hand, suggested we go directly to Rome and chain ourselves to the gates of the Vatican until the Pope interceded on our behalf.

We compromised. We sent an urgent and detailed fax transmission to our Toronto agent asking that she make things right or rebate our monies, thereby sending us on a busman's holiday in Italy. (Yes, the castle had a fax machine. Friends give me a strange look when I tell them this, but then I explain that it was one of the very first fax machines operated by two mules walking around in a circle and, yes, the ink actually does go through the phone lines!)

Three things happened immediately. We were transferred to a large villa, the one we were supposed to get in the first place, the one with a fireplace, two bedrooms, two bathrooms, a kitchen, and a living area.

The Italian property agent in Florence agreed to send a new tennis net down to Modanella forthright. And lastly, we fell in love with Tuscany, which made all the other snafus tolerable.

We verily threw ourselves at the mercy of enchanted Tuscany — we hiked, we biked, we toured, we tippled. The rented car gave us the mobility to do a day-trip to the magnificent red, round city of Siena; to San Gimignano, a walled paradise matched only in beauty by the artist's depiction of the town on the local ceramics; to medieval Montepulciano, still the seductive prize it was when Florence and Siena warred over it so many centuries ago.

We were surprised by the generosity and honesty of the handsome, fair-skinned Tuscans. Walk anywhere in the countryside and somebody will always offer you a lift. The favours were often returned with glasses of wine back at our villa. Two such saviours are now pen pals.

Proud of our Canadian resourcefulness, we got the bicycle tires pumped up in Serre di Rapolano. With a rack at each end of the embers, we barbecued steaks (believe it or not, the local Tuscan specialty) and lamb chops in our fireplace. The wash was done in the sinks and dried outside on makeshift racks.

And for sport, we adopted Italy's national pastime — bocci. Day after day, the villa management promised to produce a set of bocci balls, which never did materialize. Finally, I bought a set in Orvieto. (I know, a lot of people go there to purchase the luscious white wine!) The villa compensated me the $25 for the bocci set and kept it, so now when clients arrive and believe they must have booked a vacation from the wrong brochure, they too can run up and down the hills chasing the little pallino and arguing expressively over the score. (I also created a sport involving rocks and the carp in the ponds, but nobody else would play with me.)

The tennis net eventually arrived and spent several days in the villa's jeep before somebody put it up. We got to play one real game of tennis the day before we departed. They began to fill the pool after our initial complaint and it was ready for swimming just about the time we touched down in Toronto.

But the success of all travel adventures is measured, I think, in negatives. The fighting in the former Yugoslavia did not spill over into northern Italy, nobody lost their luggage, nobody died, and except for some feelings, nobody got hurt.

I would certainly return to Tuscany on a villa vacation, but I'd be a lot more curious about the agent. You gotta ask a lot of questions beginning with "Have you yourself personally, recently, actually, while in a waking state been there?" and ending with "Okay, there's a pool, but is there water in the pool?"

The Rapolano
Bean Field War

WHILE PREPARING FOR A MONTH'S STAY IN ITALY, THERE WAS AN ABUN-
dance of dire warnings from people who have been there recently.

They'll rob you blind, they said, steal your luggage, lift your wallet, rip off your bag from a moving motorcycle.

And I'm sure the waves of crime are ever-rising in the big cities
like Toronto . . . sorry, Taranto, Naples, Rome, Milan, etc. But in the
small villages we frequented, particularly the exquisite and elevated
Tuscan village of Serre di Rapolano, thirty minutes southeast of Siena,
honesty was the rule of daily life.

Many people in Rapolano leave their keys in the doors all day long.
Some never lock them at all. At the local *alimenteria*, loaves of fresh
bread not picked up by the afternoon closing would be placed in the
windowsill outside with the customers' names written on the bags.
Needless to say, as innocent Canadians travelling abroad, we had free
bread for the whole time we were there! (I'm kidding.)

I was so impressed, I proposed this "open door" honesty policy
when I got home to Wainfleet, but the problem is if people out here
leave their front doors open, they fear people from Dunnville will come
in and steal the chickens. (Still kidding.)

All four of us happened to be in Serre di Rapolano during Serre
Maggio, their May festival, and we found ourselves at the Spagheteria,
a temporary restaurant serving local wines, produce, and, of course,
pasta.

At that time, I knew only one person in the town — Chach, the
region's sole cab driver, and he happened to be there. With the wine
flowing freely, Chach and I had a grand old conversation, neither
understanding a word of the other's language. As best I could

understand, Chach had to go because he's been having trouble with his "undici," which I could only guess had been riding up on him. Either that or he had to pick up his eleven-year-old nephew from Sea Cadets. Great guy, Chach.

There were a lot of young people eating at these long, papered benches set up only at festival time. Most were couples who looked to be engaged or newly married. After the meal, they began what appeared to be some sort of Maggio tradition, gently tossing frecette at each other. Frecette are long, fat green beans that come into season in May.

I tried to question Chach about this strange custom, but this time his "undici" were apparently "novanta," which I took to mean in a strangle-hold position.

Anyway, the four of us watched this childish behaviour until it escalated to the point where, for the sake of common civility, something had to be done. They had begun peppering the waitress with these green beans every time she came into the room to clean them off the floor. So I — and I think you'll be proud of me on this one — sized up the situation, stood up slowly, holding a frecette to get their attention, and nailed the little guy with the glasses right on the noggin. As they say, when three hours north of Rome, do as the Rapolanos do.

What happened after that shot was fired was something out of the movies: *The Rapolano Bean Field War* meets Fellini's *8-1/2 Minutes of Veggie Madness*. Green beans rained down on us as if the Jolly Green Giant had snapped like a disgruntled U.S. postal worker. I could not, indeed I would not, stand to see our women pelted with these green missiles, which is why I had no choice but to crouch down under the table behind them and close my eyes.

It was at this point that Monica, a friend I've always known to be rational and self-controlled, grabbed the broom from the waitress and a serving tray from a nearby table, and — I'm not exaggerating here — jumped up on our long table and began a menacing march towards the enemy's table across the room.

The sight of this petite blonde, shielding herself from flying frecette with the tray in her left hand and threatening them with the broom, spear-like in her right hand, shocked everyone into a silent ceasefire. The waitress quietly backed out of the room in fear. The young couples were only stunned while we three Canadians looked up at our travel companion with mouths open, practically drooling in disbelief.

And then Monica, victory within her grasp, made a terrible tactical mistake. She did a quick two-step, twirled the broom, and began singing "Volare." Loudly.

That's when the place went nuts. That's when the young Rapolanos and the three Canadians, with gooey green paste in our hair, realized we had a common enemy. That's when everybody, including the waitress with the manager in tow, grabbed every single frecette off the floor and hit this woman repeatedly and from all sides. Nobody sings a bad "Volare" in Italy and lives.

When she refused to quit, we all just got up and left. Not a bad idea when you think about it — send this woman accompanied by an accordion player on a world tour of civil-war sites.

A week of Whoa Whoa Whoa Whoas and there won't be enough pens in the free world to sign the peace treaties.

I felt a little guilty starting this whole fiasco, but to tell you the truth, after ten hours in an airline seat, six hours on a train, and three in a car, I don't mind telling you — my undici weren't all that comfortable either.

Abroad, We're All Ambassadors

AT THE TOP OF THE WORLD, PERCHED PRECARIOUSLY ON THE SIDE OF A mountain overlooking Italy's most pristine and precious lake, sits the Hotel Zanzanu.

Like a sentry sitting watch over Lake Garda, the Hotel Zanzanu is surrounded on three sides by vineyards and cherry orchards with lakeside views of tiny mountain villages across the water, the Dolomites off in the distance, the Alps even higher and farther to the north. The Hotel Zanzanu is quite capably managed by Mr. Zambiasi. (Yes, I know what you're thinking — if they had a head waiter named Zoro and a big-breasted table dancer named Zsa-Zsa, they could call the place Club Zed!)

I had the pleasure of a one-week stay at the Hotel Zanzanu in May, playing tennis, stealing cherries, and travelling around Lake Garda on a slow ferry that stops at all the towns from Desenzano in the south to Riva in the north. Whereas many lakes in Europe are dead or dying, Lake Garda is pristine. Some say they drink the water from Lake Garda by dipping a cup in it.

I had planned to stay only a couple of days, but it took one whole week to figure the damn place out.

Somehow word got out in the hotel that I was a writer, and a meeting was hastily arranged, because the Hotel Zanzanu and other inns in the area are very keen on attracting Canadian visitors. (Gee, I can't imagine why. The orders that their German guests bark out are so crisp and clear!) Anyway, they wanted my opinion on how best to attract Canadian tourists to the Garda area because — and I hope you're sitting down for this one — people in other countries actually respect writers. (I didn't let on that my particular field of expertise as a writer was making fun of my ex-wife's brother, my mother, and my cat. So if you go there, please keep this information to yourself. That and the part about me owning Air Canada. Thank you.)

After being tossed out of that Cuban cemetery, I've tried hard to be a better tourist, wearing my little Canadian flag pin with pride and on anything that doesn't have mustard stains. So I was determined to make a good impression at this summit, which was chaired by the gracious and engaging Signore Zambiasi and sponsored exclusively by Campari on ice.

So there's four of us: me, Mr. Zambiasi, a happy-go-lucky guy whom I know to be the hotel plumber, and Gian Pietro Chiesa, the marketing manager for the local hotel association and a man who looks exactly like Leonardo da Vinci's illegitimate great-great-great-grandson Johnny. It was dimly lit, with Italian stringed instruments straining in the background. Just imagine that restaurant scene in *Godfather II* just before Michael goes to the bathroom and finds the gun in the toilet — and you've got it.

I begin the meeting by complimenting Mr. Collini on the great job he's been doing on the leaking water pipe near the tennis court, when Mr. Zambiasi informs me that Signore Collini is the owner of the hotel.

"I love a man who does his own plumbing," I added quickly, but everybody just stared at the table.

Signore Collini begins to tell me the legend of Zanzanu, a sixteenth-century pirate who stole from the rich . . .

"Yeah, like Mr. Zambiasi was saying — " I interrupted him just to let him know I'd already been told the story.

But Mr. Collini only understood the first couple of words of English. Immediately he turned to Gian Pietro and said, "Signore Zambiasi is stealing from me?" Blank stares all around.

I admit, this wasn't much of a recovery from the plumber crack.

At this point, had anybody made a move for the john, I'd have raced in first and thoroughly searched the toilet.

Switching from translator to referee, Gian Pietro jumped in to calm everybody down.

If you ever wonder why the United Nations doesn't work, sit down sometime and conduct a four-way conversation using bits and pieces of three languages. Then, when things couldn't get any worse, add alcohol.

Anyway, I finally got to introduce some special requests that Canadians travelling to the Hotel Zanzanu might really enjoy.

Light beer.

"Light beer?" they asked.

"Yes," I said. "Take all that wonderful rich German and Italian beer, water it down, but charge us the same price. It's a Canadian tradition." They wrote it down.

Television sets at each end of the bar with non-stop sportscasts.

"But it's a quiet bar with classical music playing," they said.

"Perfect," I replied. "Crank up the volume, turn the sound off on the television sets, and put a jukebox in the corner blaring out Garth Brooks's greatest hits. It's the Canadian way." They nodded.

"And put 50% Off signs all over the place."

"Cut our prices by half!" they protested.

"No. Leave your prices exactly as they are," I said. "Just put 50% Off signs everywhere. Canadians will gladly pay full price as long as they think they're getting a deal."

"A Canadian tradition?" they asked.

"Our secret to economic security," I replied.

A few other innovations I was able to negotiate on your behalf, should you choose to stay at the Hotel Zanzanu: horseshoe pits in the vineyard, jet skis in the pool, and more stealable toiletries in the rooms.

You're welcome.

The meeting ended shortly after they asked me what Canadians thought of Italian politics. I recalled the story about the Italian cabinet minister who, while leaving for lunch, tells his secretary that if the prime minister calls, to take a message. Then, as an afterthought, he sticks his head back in the door and says: "And get his name."

This went over very well. There were laughs all around.

Then they asked me about the best Canadian political joke. I said, at the moment, it was Preston Manning. I don't think they got it. On that note, the meeting was adjourned.

Somehow I don't see an ambassadorship in my future.

I have a sneaking suspicion that the United States sent someone just like me to smooth things over with Saddam, just before Desert Storm.

The Man Who Danced with His Luggage

THE PAST SIX YEARS I'VE MADE IT A SPRING RITUAL TO SPEND A MONTH OR so in Europe. I've done this for you, the reader, because I feel it's important to know once and for all who is weirder — us or the Europeans. At this time, I'm pleased to reveal the results of this exhaustive study: *them*. Hands down.

Oh, sure, we've got the guy in Peterborough who enjoys crawling into the hole of campground outhouses and when women enter he . . . Well, it's kind of a form of self-inflicted mooning. As you know, they caught the guy and, boy, is he in deep . . . now.

And, yes, we've got the guy from Stetler, Alberta, who ate his underwear at a roadside breathalyzer stop believing that the cotton in the fabric would absorb the alcohol in his bloodstream and he would hence pass the test down at RCMP headquarters. Alas, wind and water were all he could pass and he was subsequently charged. The Fruit of the Loom boys were devastated. Had the process worked, it would have given a tremendous boost to their careers.

Okay, so we have some people with whom you wouldn't want to go on a long trip with in a compact automobile.

But in Lucignano, a beautiful mountain village south of Siena, I stumbled across the world's strangest musical conductor at their annual Maggio festival.

While the band played up on the stage in the main square in Lucignano, this maestro stood down in front on the dance floor, making moves that only Arthur Fiedler and the Energizer Bunny have ever made before. Although it was not officially karaoke, he flawlessly mouthed the words of every song. As I moved closer to the front of the bandstand, I noticed three things that distinguished him from,

say, Leonard Bernstein.

This maestro was conducting the orchestra with a comb he kept whipping out of his back pocket. This man was not officially part of the orchestra. The members of the orchestra, from their vantage point, did not know he was there.

When the band stopped playing a song, and there was that awkward lull in the program — you guessed it — he took that opportunity to comb his hair. This guy was definitely not a one-dimensional artist. Very deliberately the comb went back into his back pocket, he exercised and loosened up his fingers, and then, precisely on cue, he'd whip that multi-toothed baton out of his jeans just as the music started up again.

Entertaining? Myself and two Italian guys whom I'd never met before took turns holding each other up during the polka part of the program.

Yet, in the major league of weird, this does not even come close to what my brother-in-law Danny still claims is the greatest moment in his sad but eventful life.

The last night of our great misadventure to Portugal, we ended up in the Rossio area of Lisbon. It was very late, but in this little square, with people hanging out their apartment windows to watch, the band played courageously on as about a dozen couples still danced around the fountain. Danny picked the spot, he told me the next day, because the guidebook stated that tourists should never go to this area of the city late at night.

The participants of what looked to be a dance marathon looked like characters Fellini would be too frightened to cast in a film. There were street toughs, pickpockets, prostitutes, construction workers still wearing their helmets, a sailor, young children, food vendors, candy flossers, and a well-dressed fat man who danced elegantly with his wife, who kept her eyes closed the whole time.

As the crowd gathered tight around the edge of the square and shoving matches flared up here and there, the dancers — some old men partnered with other old men — joyfully circled the fountain oblivious to anything but music. It was like a bad dream bordering on a good nightmare. It was a foreign film directed by a warped mind — uncut with no subtitles.

And then the missing masterpiece to this bizarre musical puzzle appeared, and my brother-in-law's life was complete. A little man, who had been jilted as a partner by every single woman on the square, appeared from a dark alley and, with smile of pride on his face, he began dancing — with his luggage.

Searching the faces of the crowd, we soon realized that no one but us found this unusual.

The little man continued to dance with his luggage for at least an hour, until I had to carry Danny back to our hotel and apply ice packs to his forehead.

This single, strange event scared us to the point where even now we'll get together once in a while to try to rationalize what we saw.

"It wasn't cheap luggage," Danny will say.

"Good leather," I'll respond. "Nothing synthetic about it."

"For a little guy, he could really handle that bag on the turns," Danny will say.

"It was new leather too," I'll add. "That was not an old bag he was dancing with."

"During the fast ones, they were the best couple out there," Danny will say.

"Only a technicality kept them from winning that ladies' choice spot dance," I'll say.

Any way you cut it, it's them, not us, in the Superbowl of Strange. But they definitely have a classier breed of weird.

"Darren Laitte — you come out of that outhouse this instant. Next thing we know, you'll be dragging your brother along to the two-holers!"

The Dumbest Guy in England, New Year's Day

BEFORE I LEFT FOR MY ANNUAL NEW YEAR'S VACATION, THIS TIME A HIKE across southern England, I dashed off a quick column to cover my time away. It was standard year-end stuff: the stupidest things we said in 1995. It was a good year, not a great year, for oral oops!

There was the poacher in Wausau, Wisconsin, John Sadogierski, charged with killing and eating a trumpeter swan and a sandhill crane. When asked by the arresting officer, just out of curiosity, what exactly did crane taste like, the alleged poacher immediately replied: "Bald eagle!" He was no longer "alleged." (I believe the correct answer was "chicken.")

There was the Canadian soldier accused of sexual assault in Croatia, after consuming a litre of red wine, some brandy, and between twelve and fourteen ounces of Sambuca. He described himself as "fairly drunk."

Fairly drunk? I looked it up, and according to the *Official Canadian Peacekeeper's Conduct Manual*, this kind of consumption does not constitute the condition of "fairly drunk." No, this consumption of alcohol, when accompanied by eggs, is officially known as the "Canadian Airborne Grand Slam Breakfast."

There was Judge Eugene Chambers of Houston, Texas, so frustrated by the guard who kept asking for photo I.D. every time he entered his own court, that he screamed: "Up your [deleted] with a bucket of red paint!" I'm not sure, but I believe that's how the artist Christo got started.

I had to straighten out a serious misquote sent to me by several excited males who read my column. It was a misleading radio report about the Hubble Space Telescope and photographs of a new star formation called Eagle Nebula. I hated to break their hearts, but I tracked the story down and determined the word in question was *tips*, quote: "a new shape with *tips* larger than our solar system."

And finally, there were the haunting words of a true believer at Christmastime, the woman who called a pet specialty shop in Buffalo, New York, to order a sweater for her poodle. The sweaters were in stock, great. The price was mentioned, no problem. Then the dog's size was requested. When she admitted she had no idea, the pet-store person told her to take a measuring tape and get the dog's height, length, and girth.

"Oh, no," she replied, "I couldn't do that. I want this to be a surprise."

I filed the column of quirky quotes and boarded a flight for London feeling fairly certain I had chronicled some of the dumbest things we've done and said for a while to come. Little did I know it, they were merely the preliminaries and I was headed for the world championships.

Sure, you can ask: just why would I go to England for a New Year's holiday in the midst of the coldest snowstorm they've had on record? Because I was too cheap to purchase cancellation insurance. No more questions.

Snow, ice, freezing rain — "get the critters out," they kept demanding in the pubs, as people watched highway disaster clips on the telly.

"No, no!" I protested, "I'm Canadian. I know about these things. Keep the critters indoors or they'll freeze their little bums off!"

For the record, when the English are faced with hazardous icy roads, they call for the sanders, or as they call them, "gritters."

So how was my quick trip to Merry Ol'? Well, except for the fact that I can't seem to stop saying "a bit dodgy, that," it was . . . "oh, spot on, Seth, spot on." "Wot? DoyouknowhatImean?"

For the most part, I walked for five days along the coast of southern England, from Seaford to Bournemouth, with a woman who was supposed to take photos but didn't because "she forgot her woollies, she did." We have great shots of fireplaces in pubs.

Actually, we missed the worst of the storm and managed to walk about sixteen miles a day with backpacks along the beaches and cliffs of the English Channel. From that vantage point, on a clear day, with binoculars, you can see right across to France, and even at that distance, if they know you're watching, the French will exhibit rude behaviour.

I spent New Year's Eve on the Isle of Wight, in the Metropole Hotel, which was a beautiful seaside inn — sometime back in the 1940s, I'm sure. Today it's locked in a losing race with the wrecking ball.

Standing on our balcony, sipping champagne, our entertainment for the night was as follows: the surf of the English Channel crashing into the wall below and soaking party-goers as they walked by, two women fist-fighting in front of the Mill Bay Pub next door, and Bob. Bob, a boyfriend of one of the lady wrestlers, stood in front of us taunting the pub's bouncer, from 1995 to 1996. Bob had so many rings pierced through so many body parts that had I not wanted to see the new year so much, I would have run down and fitted him with our shower curtain.

But the next day we discovered the stupidest guy in all of England, at least on New Year's Day.

We had hiked out of Ventnor headed south along the coast of the Isle of Wight, and after five hours on the footpath, we decided to get a bus to Yarmouth and from there a ferry back to the mainland.

No buses — everything on the Isle shuts down on New Year's Day.

So we began hitchhiking and before too long got picked up by a young English couple in their small compact car.

I've been to London and the British Isles a half a dozen times, but I keep forgetting how terribly friendly and helpful the British really are. I'm sitting in the back seat, on the passenger side, and the young chap, sorry, the guy is sitting in the front left where he's supposed to be. I cannot see his wife sitting directly in front of me because my back-pack is on my lap. This bloke, sorry, this guy is fascinated that we're just out hiking and hitching with no real destination or booked accommodation. In a country with a pub every mile,

94

if not every block, I wouldn't say we were exactly roughing it.

He asked a lot of questions, but the problem was he turned right around to face me when he asked them. We were having a great animated conversation, but his eyes were rarely on the road.

England, as you may know, is a country where hedges line the rural routes so cars coming out of the side roads have to nose out onto the thoroughfare before the driver can see both ways. Every time a car edged out in front of us, I gently pushed the guy's arm and pointed out the problem because mostly he was facing me and not the oncoming motorcar just ahead that was about to end all our lives. I began to sweat.

Each time I'd point out a potential danger, he'd say, "No fear, mate," and turn around to talk to us again, and as nicely as I could, I'd urge him to look up ahead where an oncoming lorry, sorry, truck was headed straight for us and carrying four coffins with our respective names embossed on the sides. Now I'm breathing hard and answering all his questions with: "Yeah, sure."

Anyway, this went on until my forehead beaded up and he began looking at me as though I was in his country recovering from bad brain surgery.

Finally, the car stopped and we departed with a polite "Cheers."

That's when I said to my travelling companion: "That bleedin' bounder, sorry, that freakin' lunatic nearly got us killed. The man's a maniac! He only looked at the road when I drew his attention to it!"

That's when my travelling partner turned to me and said, and with a certain amount of merit, I must admit: "He wasn't driving, stupid. She was."

Why in the hell can't these people put the steering wheel on the right side, that is the correct side, I mean the left side? A bit patchy that, Seth. Wot? DoyouknowwhatImean?

Okay, so England's first moron of the first month of 1996 was an import. I have a valid passport. I had a right to be there!

PART III

Non-Excellent Adventures

Men Really Strut Their Stuff in March

I CANNOT TELL YOU WHY, BUT NO MONTH BETTER EXEMPLIFIES THE MISADventures of men than March. Call it cabin fever, call it the bad dream weaver, call it what you want — it's one strange stretch of time. Take March 1994.

That's the month kids in Whistler, B.C., were charged with cursing in public, while in Quebec, mass murderer Denis Lortie was set free. Apparently, *he* said he was sorry.

Native Canadians were still occupying a Revenue Canada building in Toronto, but they quit and went home when they could muster no public support for their cause.

Not real bright, guys. You want support? You want cheering in the street? Next time you occupy a Revenue Canada building, give us a toll-free number to call: 1-800-BURN-MY-FILE.

Just down the road, a thirty-three-year-old man robbed the Port Colborne Credit Union where I bank and tried to escape on a bicycle, in fresh March snow. Lacking snow tires, the robber made his getaway walking beside the bicycle, thus producing both footprints and tire tracks in the snow. One bystander followed the robber on foot and told a passing motorist to call police. Another man, a bank customer, alerted the bank manager, and they set out following the robber in a car.

Police response time was not what it should have been because they couldn't break through the parade of people following the robber. Most townsfolk watched the procession thinking the St. Patrick's Day Parade was rather subdued this year. The robber was arrested in a back yard that wasn't his, sitting in a hot tub that wasn't on, counting money that, in part, belonged to me. Police are not calling this the Great Escape.

The small town has had two hostage-taking standoffs in its history. The first was last March, and now, twelve months later, yet another lonely guy with a loaded gun kept police at bay for seven hours — in the same apartment building. The standoff ended when police broke his bedroom window and woke the gunman up. It doesn't seem fair. I've had a lot of difficulty sleeping lately, yet here's a guy surrounded by thirty sharpshooters who have him in their crosshairs and he's out like a light.

Two armed standoffs in the history of Port Colborne in the same small apartment building! I have one word for the super — *references!*

In Ontario, a long list of educational reforms proposed to the government included standardized testing, full-day kindergarten, and the abolition of grade 13. The proposal by federal MP Jag Bhaduria to "line principals up against the wall and shoot them" is not expected to pass on first reading.

A Norwegian man, mowing lawns near Oslo, was charged with drunk driving when police stopped his lawnmower in a spot check. (This report has no comedic value in Norway, a country unfamiliar with the term *half-cut*.)

After 17 years, 632 lessons, 8 instructors, and 5 crashes, David Guest of London, England, finally passed his driving test. In all modesty, he claimed his main problem was confusing the clutch with the brake. That defence never worked for Thelma and Louise.

"I bent down on my knees and thanked God," he said when told he'd passed. So did I when I learned David has no plans for a motorcar tour of Canada. Give this guy a few distractions like a car phone, a dashboard fax machine, and some talking tapes and he'll wreak more havoc on England than the militant wing of the IRA.

Bill Passingham, one hundred years old, was still driving the streets of St. Catharines, Ontario, in March, having passed his mandatory driver's test a couple of months earlier. Bill recalled his great disappointment at failing his very first test at age sixteen, when while he was trying to parallel park, his horse tripped and fell backwards over the curb.

In March, a news report from Columbia, South Carolina, described an incident in which a cow stepped on a rifle in a field and it discharged, shooting another cow. No valuables were found to be missing from the victim cow and the police still have no motive.

Near North Bay, Ontario, a tourist from France who mistakenly believed his trip from Ottawa to Vancouver would take two hours instead of three days created quite a scene and was thrown from a Greyhound bus and killed. Greyhound wants passengers to know they are very strict when it comes to departure and arrival times. Please keep this in mind as Greyhound moves into the airline business.

And just north of Toronto, the month of March gave us what has to be the unluckiest soul of the entire year. A forty-one-year-old drifter was hit by a train and killed while walking on the tracks in Vaughan on Monday, March 20. That particular Monday was the first day of Canada's railroad strike. The rail line that runs from Vaughan to Toronto is a non-unionized line and the only railway in the country with a train running on it that day.

It's a very big country. I mean, really, what are the chances?

Still not convinced that March is the most mysterious month of the year? How about this. Do you ever remember a time when baseball and railroads were on strike and the post office wasn't?

In Search of the Naked Truth

I N MAN'S UNREQUITED QUEST TO FIND TRUE MEANING IN LIFE, THERE is always the danger of taking the advice of our leaders a little too literally.

A good example is the recent incident in which twenty church people from Floydada, Texas, who heard the Lord tell them "to get rid of all their belongings and go to Louisiana" were arrested a few days later in Vinton, Louisiana, starkers!

I can't tell you how shocked I was when I read about this. I thought to myself: twenty buck-naked religious people in one vehicle — good Lord, the Doukhobors are car pooling!

Explained Vinton Police Chief Dennis Drouillard: "They got rid of all their clothes and pocketbooks and wallets and identification and the licence plate off their car and came to our gorgeous state." This, I believe, illustrates the depths to which American society has sunk. Facing twenty naked lawbreakers, the chief still couldn't resist a shameless plug for his home state. (New motto: Church People Welcome. Free Loincloths!)

Chief Drouillard had never seen twenty nudes in one car, mainly because he has never served on the Fort Lauderdale police force during spring break.

Twenty naked people travelling 550 miles in a 1990 Pontiac Grand Am (and you have to hope the Lord also told them "No tickling!") not only creates a real challenge at toll booths, it also makes those roadside stop snacks pretty dicey as well. It's not as if they could flip a coin to see who goes in to get the burgers. Nobody's got pockets!

Self-serve gas stations are out of the question, and it's highly unlikely you'll find attendants willing to blindfold themselves before they clean the windshield.

Driver and Pentecostal preacher Sammy Rodriguez was arrested in Vinton when he drove the car into a tree while being pursued by police. Rodriguez did not offer an explanation for the accident, but it's possible he was distracted by the advice of nineteen naked backseat drivers. The real puzzler for me was that nobody was charged for not wearing a seatbelt, or even mooning the scene of an accident.

And another thing I wondered about: do you think buck-naked drivers wave to one another like guys who drive MGs?

Somewhere in the state of Louisiana today, a hitchhiker lies on a chiropractor's couch with a badly wrenched neck. Having been told the story of how it happened, the chiropractor is trying to persuade him to go next door and see the psychiatrist.

I don't have to tell you, the pro-clothing segment of society, that this kind of behaviour must be stopped and stopped now before Ralph Nader forces General Motors to recall all 1990 Pontiac Grand Ams and replace the dual air bags with twenty pairs of flannel pajamas.

Although this episode reflects very favourably on the roominess of the Pontiac Grand Am, I'm not sure General Motors is all that thrilled about it. A spokesman for the car company has said that in the future, all GM dealerships are forbidden to sell convertibles to customers not wearing clothes.

Twenty religious people going stark naked in public upsets the natural order of things. To restore the balance, I believe somewhere in Louisiana twenty atheists should march through a nudist camp fully clothed. It's only fair.

The police chief of Floydada interviewed a relative who said the group "made statements like the devil was after them and Floydada was going to be destroyed if they stayed there."

Well, as tempting as that sounds, to destroy towns with really stupid-sounding names, I just don't think that's the way the devil works. Otherwise, Petawawa, Antigonish, and Punkydoodles Corners (honest, it's near Stratford, Ontario) would have been wiped out years ago.

No, this buck-naked church people movement must be nipped in the . . . must be stopped before it becomes a trend. It could have quite an impact on the local economy. I mean, what about the poor guy in Vinton who supplies churches in that town with metal pews?

The moral of this story is that the words of our leaders must be taken with a grain of salt or in the case of twenty naked Pentecostals, a grain of saltpeter. Blind faith is always dangerous, if not deadly.

Just look at our political leaders in Canada. If they said to us, we're all going to jump off a cliff and we want you to jump with us, are we going to say, why yes of course, O great leaders?

No, of course not. What we're going to say is sure — you first.

Daredevils of the Mighty Niagara

Niagara Falls, Honeymoon Capital of the World. They talk about marriages made in heaven. Well, this is where they test-drive them.

For almost a hundred years men, real men, have come to Niagara Falls to defy the might of Mother Nature, to challenge its raging torrent of water, to lay their lives on the line that drops dramatically 164 feet straight down into a churning canyon of angry currents. I tell you, these are men with nerves of steel. These are men with hearts of lions. These, ladies and gentlemen, are men with shit for brains.

Most men have an instinctive need to impress other men. The daredevils of Niagara harbour a need to impress a special breed of men. They're called coroners.

(Writer's note: For men in a weakened state of mind thinking of taking the leap, Niagara Falls can be a death trap. But, right now, I'd like to stick to the topic of daredevils. I'll deal with marriage in a chapter that follows this one.)

Here, then, is the highlight reel of daredevils who have gone over Niagara Falls.

In 1989, American Jessie Sharp went over Niagara Falls in a white-water kayak. Like all daredevils, Jessie had high hopes of fame and riches. He told the media before he went over that he had planned the trip over Niagara Falls for ten long years. The trip over the falls took 4.5 seconds. Niagara Parks Police found the body a few days later. Experts believe this stunt was way, way over-planned.

Dave Mundy from Caistor Centre, Ontario, went over the falls in a barrel in 1985 and lived. Several summers ago Dave attempted to shoot Niagara Falls again, but his barrel got grounded at the brink of the falls and he had to be rescued with a crane. Dave is determined to try again and has stated that if he succeeds, for his next trick he'd really like to fly an airplane into a bus. You might remember that the next time you're in Niagara Falls and thinking about taking public transit. My advice: if you find yourself on a bus in Niagara Falls being tailgated by an airplane piloted by a guy wrapped in air bags and wearing a hockey helmet — get off at the next stop.

My own personal favourite is Peter deBernardi, who went over the falls in a two-man barrel with Jeffrey Petrovitch, September 27, 1989. They survived. Afterwards, when asked why he did it, Peter said: "To show kids there are better things to do than drugs!"

Not to argue with Peter's logic, but I'm trying to imagine the choice: "Okay, Jimmy, you can smoke this joint of marijuana or get inside that metal ball over there, we'll seal you in so you have about a half-hour's worth of air, then you'll come bobbing down that raging river at 70 miles per hour, drop 164 feet in 4.5 seconds under 212,000 cubic feet of pressure, and the chances of you dying are very, very good."

I don't know about you, son, but I think Jimmy might say something like: "Uh . . . you got one of those roach clips so I don't burn my fingers?"

Over a decade ago, Karel Souchek of Hamilton, Ontario, beat the odds and lived. After twice going through the Lower Rapids of Niagara Falls in a barrel, Karel went head-on with the Horseshoe Falls on July 2, 1984. I interviewed Karel for a magazine story and concluded that he had a strong desire to be famous — along with a nagging death wish. This is a bad combination in the business of stunting. Karel was a media hound, alerting reporters to the time of his impending stunt for maximum coverage. For instance, he'd call and say he was going over Saturday and if you said you were out of town Saturday, Karel would say: "Okay. What are you doing Monday?"

Like all successful daredevils, Karel did not receive the recognition he'd hoped for. Consequently, a year later, Karel attempted to recreate his Niagara Falls feat in a stunt exhibition at the Houston Astrodome. Honest. They sealed Karel up in the same barrel he'd used at the falls and dropped him from a ceiling platform, 175 feet above a large tank of water. Unfortunately, the barrel hit the side of the tank and Karel was killed instantly, proving once and for all that going over Niagara Falls in a barrel is not an indoor sport!

For me, the most interesting stunt was that of Steven Trotter and Lori Martin of Columbus, Georgia. Steven went over the falls solo in 1985, and in June of 1994 the two of them went over in a double barrel. Amazingly, the woman who had planned and practised with Steven to shoot the falls chickened out at the last minute. Lori Martin was an eleventh-hour replacement. I can only imagine how this happened.

Steven: "So, Lori, I'm leaving for Canada in the morning and I was wondering, would you like to come along, do a little sightseeing, a candlelight dinner overlooking the falls, and then we could, well . . . you know . . .

Slap! Lori: "You pig! You're just like all the rest of them. You have just one thing —"

Steven: "Oh no, Lori. After dinner, I thought we might get into a barrel and go over Niagara Falls, a thrilling but extremely dangerous stunt in which we might both be killed or badly injured."

Lori: "Oh, okay. For a minute there I thought you were trying to get physical."

I know guys who have tried unsuccessfully for years to get their wives to go fishing with them, but this, this is incredible.

Immediately after the stunt, the Niagara Parks Police seized Trotter's barrel and he was later fined $5,500.

Trotter's stunt took place on Father's Day, and he dedicated the whole adventure as a gift to his father, who was at the falls and watching. Fortunately, the couple weren't killed. We all know what a bummer it is to have to collect your Father's Day gift at the morgue.

A fascinating pattern has developed in the hundred years that daredevils have been defying the falls. Only one woman, Annie Edson Taylor, successfully shot the falls solo, in 1901, and no woman has tried since.

But thirteen men have made the trip and four of them have died! Guys! Exactly how many dead daredevils does it take to convince you that going over Niagara Falls in a barrel is not such a neat idea?

The world's largest zucchini is located at the Guinness Book of World Records Museum on Clifton Hill. And you're probably saying to yourself: Gee, Bill, what does a large zucchini have to do with the daredevils of Niagara?

To my mind, everything.

If Your Wife Has a Fu Manchu, Be Very, Very Afraid

THE DILEMMA OF THE MARRIED MAN IN THE '90S DEEPENS ALMOST DAILY AS children turn to crime, the Internet turns to pornography and bomb-making, and the wife turns away from you in the shower so as not to reveal her male private parts.

Yes, by now you've heard of a guy named Bruce Jensen of Bountiful, Utah, who feels "pretty stupid" about discovering that his wife of three and one-half years is, in fact, a man. The news report I'm looking at has a photograph of Bruce's thirty-four-year-old wife, Felix Urioste.

Uh, Bruce, I have to tell you, if the first name Felix is not at least a tipoff, that thick black Fu Manchu moustache sets a little bird off in my brain screaming: DEAD GIVEAWAY, BILL. DEAD GIVEAWAY.

Authorities said Urioste got away with the deception because he looked feminine and never let Bruce see him naked during their marriage. Oddly enough, I believe those were the same two reasons given by Tom Arnold on why his marriage to Roseanne Barr lasted as long as it did.

Urioste got Bruce to marry when he (the wife) claimed he (now the mother) was pregnant with his (the husband's) twins after a single sexual encounter in 1991, the likes of which could cause irreparable harm to your imagination if you even try to think about it.

Bruce, thirty-nine years old, became even more distressed when he discovered his two children by a previous marriage, Jughead and his younger brother Archie, are in fact cardboard cutouts. (Okay, I made that part up.)

Actually, Felix (the bride with a lot to blush about) entrapped Bruce (the gullible groom) into marriage, then quickly claimed the twins were stillborn.

From conception to the miracle of childbirth, you've probably noticed Bruce has shown an unusual lack of curiosity, even for a guy. A shame, really, because with this unique span of attention, Bruce could have been an O.J. juror and been on the book tour by now.

Bruce is now seeking an annulment of the marriage, citing irreconcilable similarities — sorry, differences. I say let them arm-wrestle for the matrimonial property, provided trained technicians are standing by to prevent another unwanted pregnancy.

I think it's important that we learn something from the matrimonial misadventures of Bruce: "Hey, honey? Did you talk to the TV repairman about leaving those empty beer cans under the couch again?"

Okay. So just in case you have reason to be skeptical, here are twelve surefire signs your wife might in fact be a man.

1. You found a sales slip that shows she exchanged the box of Turtles you gave her for Valentine's Day for a box of Monte Cristos.

2. She never criticizes your driving.

3. She says she's going to the movies with the girls, but asks to borrow your catcher's mitt and protective cup.

4. You notice she's always borrowing your razor and her legs are always hairy.

5. The last time you both attended a stag and doe party, she wore the antlers.

6. She belches and scratches herself when your family comes to dinner.

7. She yells "YUK!" before you do when those feminine-hygiene ads come on TV.

8. She inadvertently passes the phone to you when the telemarketer asks to speak to the "woman of the house."

9. You can't seem to keep a box of Kleenex in the house and nobody ever gets colds.

10. She finds a job for you to do in the garage every time *Baywatch* comes on TV.

11. She regularly runs onto construction sites and beats the hell out of guys who whistle at her.

And, gentlemen, here's where the little bird in the brain should start screaming DEAD GIVEAWAY!

12. She's never nagged you.

"Throw Down Your Can Opener and Come Out with Your Hands Up!"

I WAS DEEPLY DISTRESSED LAST WEEK WHEN I HEARD AN AMERICAN RADIO broadcast detailing the misfortune of a man from Calgary who today sits in a jail in western Canada. Some days it just doesn't pay to get out of bed, and on this day, twenty-one-year-old Patrick O'Connor definitely should have hit the snooze button. But if he had, he probably would have cut himself. It seems O'Connor tried to rob a grocery store in Calgary and, but for two serious mistakes, he may well have pulled it off.

Mistake No. 1 — Patrick ignored the most common weapon of choice used by retail robbers, that is, a weapon. Instead, Patrick tried to hold up the store with a can opener.

Well, this hardly ever happens in the robbery business, and so it comes as no surprise that the clerk was not intimidated by the can opener and did not respond immediately to Patrick's demand for money. It's quite likely the clerk had the same hunch I have — that the can opener wasn't loaded.

Details of the event being somewhat sketchy, I can only imagine that Patrick's threat of violence went something like: "Give me all the money or I'll open every tin of Chef Boyardee in the store!"

I'd like to think it wasn't Patrick's fault. I'd like to think that he actually purchased an Uzi submachine gun, but some unscrupulous gunshop owner slipped a can opener into his shopping bag after the deal was done. Instead of going home to practise with his new firearm, Patrick went straight to the grocery store and, well . . . it was definitely the wrong tool for the job. As it turned out, so was Patrick.

Maybe it was a mistake. Maybe Patrick knew he was armed only with a can opener, but he actually intended on robbing the Canadian Imperial Pantry of Commerce.

The police report did not clarify whether Patrick was armed with a hand-operated can opener or an electric can opener. I only hope he did not embarrass himself by asking the store clerk to plug the damn thing in before he made his holdup demand. Any weapon (and professional robbers, I think, will agree with me) that must be plugged into a wall socket severely limits your range of operation. And of course there's always the risk that somebody (say, Patrick) might trip over the cord and hurt himself.

Mistake No. 2 — Patrick, being a solid family-type guy, brought the daughter of his girlfriend along for the robbery. At just sixteen months of age (and mothers, I think, will agree with me), a child cannot always be counted on to behave in a grocery store. So after Patrick brought the house down with his can-opener routine and was making good his getaway, the toddler kept climbing out of her baby carriage, costing him valuable escape time.

More so than any other crime ever committed, this was a robbery in need of progress.

Consequently, Patrick (and I'm sure you're going to be as surprised as I was) was caught and arrested by Calgary police for attempted robbery.

It's strictly a discretionary call on the part of the police, but I found it interesting that they charged Patrick with attempted robbery and not possession of a deadly kitchen utensil. The latter is the more serious charge, punishable with a mandatory ten years in a maximum-security kitchen.

Apparently, police in that city were not thrown off the track by the rather unusual and daring use of a baby carriage as a getaway vehicle.

Patrick did not resist arrest, which avoided an ugly scene of sharp-shooters on nearby rooftops and a police captain with a megaphone yelling: "Throw down your can opener and come out with your hands up!"

Police did not charge the child. I suppose there's some sort of law in that province that no person can be considered an accessory to armed robbery while they're still teething. Prosecutors plan to call the child as a witness once she learns how to talk.

Why Patrick brought the child along on the holdup is still unclear, but I suppose he's smart enough to understand that every successful robbery needs a mastermind. Psychiatrists required to submit a report on Patrick's competency to stand trial say that when they took the proverbial look into this criminal's mind, they saw a neon sign flashing "Vacancy! Vacancy!"

Though Patrick's modus operandi lacked a certain amount of preparation and attention to detail, there's hope. In jail, Patrick will learn from seasoned criminals who will school him in all the areas in which he's having problems. Like delivery of demand.

"No, no, Patrick, it's not 'I got a gub.' It's a *gun*. Let's try it again. 'I got a gun and I want your . . .' Come on . . . No, not honey. *Money*, Patrick, *money*."

I suppose most people thought it was kind of stupid of Patrick O'Connor to try to rob a store with a can opener. Most people, that is, except Vera Williams, seventy-three, from New Brunswick, who, according to another news report, was arrested recently for assaulting an RCMP officer with a toy badminton racquet. (And no, she was not aiming for his bird.)

I've said it before and I'll say it again — how are we supposed to compete with the Americans if we don't have access to the proper technology?

A Guy's Guide to the Canadian Unity Crisis

O N THE EVENING OF OCTOBER 30, 1995, REFERENDUM NIGHT, LIKE SEVEN million other Canadians I turned on my television set to watch the results. Unfortunately, I tuned in to CHCH-TV in Hamilton, Ontario.

And bless their red maple leaf hearts, on this, the most important single evening in our nation's history, CHCH-TV was broadcasting *Monday Night Football*.

Not for a minute am I suggesting CHCH-TV is unpatriotic. No, what happened was CHCH-TV, in anticipating a Yes victory and the eventual armed takeover of Canada by U.S. Marines, aired an American football game to scout for free agents in the event the Hamilton Tiger Cats would one day play in the National Football League. (Please, would somebody award this city a major league sports franchise before they sell Copps Coliseum out for a full season of dwarf tossing!)

But that's not the problem. The problem was that during the entire game, CHCH-TV ran a ribbon across the bottom of the television screen showing the referendum vote count. The problem is, they confused the hell out of guys in bars watching their local station (which I admit is not all that hard to do). The problem is that even today there are guys walking around the city of Hamilton with stupid looks on their faces because they believe they witnessed a game in which the Chicago Bears beat the Minnesota Vikings 50.6 to 49.4. (I, on the other hand, clued in after the first quarter, when the score was 52.3 to 47.7.)

Many guys feel that with the score so close, the fair thing to do would be to play ten minutes of sudden death overtime.

In fairness, they're not the only people confused about referendum events. On Sunday, Toronto staged a car rally in support of the No side, linking cars bumper-to-bumper along Highway 401 from

Toronto to Montreal. Great idea, eh? Everybody east of Toronto who saw the chain of cars and heard the horns honking had no idea it was a patriotic gesture extended to Quebec. They just thought it was Monday. I love this country — Quebec is fighting for its very existence and Toronto sends in a traffic jam.

So to clear up the confusion about the Bears' 50.6 to 49.4 victory over the Vikings, let me explain to guys who drink and watch CHCH-TV what really happened.

You see, on that particular Monday night there was a referendum on Quebec separation and . . . Quebec. It's east of here. You know when you're driving to Kingston and you're not paying attention when suddenly you start to see signs for "Patates Frites"? Yeah, that's the place. So they were thinking of separating, but they never really called it separation and the No vote was really saying "yes" to Canada and the Yes vote was "no" to Confederation and . . .

Forget all that. Here it is. Pay attention. Late in the fourth quarter, Kevin Butler kicked a field goal for the Bears and only half the ball went through the goal posts. Bears 50.6, Vikings 49.4. Let's move on.

I think it's important for the future of this country that guys in bars understand the referendum situation because, let's face it, unlike ethnics and Anglos in the province of Quebec, they have the right to vote.

So here's kind of a glossary of sports terms to help jocks get their heads around this Quebec thing:

"We really gave 110 percent out there tonight." How Francophone scrutineers in rural areas explained how there were more Yes votes than people.

"Don't pop the champagne corks yet!" The advice not heeded by Jacques Parizeau minutes before he made his now famous "screw 'em all" speech.

"It's going to be a long series. We'll just have to take it one referendum at a time." PM Jean Chrétien, who, after Meech, Charlottetown, and this last referendum, is now proposing a best four out of seven series involving the Leafs, the Canadiens, and wild card entries.

"I guess we were a little behind the eight ball." Also Jean Chrétien, just before the eight ball of unity rolled over and flattened him.

"You bunch of funny-looking, googly-eyed, thick-tongued . . ." Sorry, that had nothing to do with the referendum. That was overheard at a strategy session on multiculturalism attended by Lucien Bouchard, Jacques Parizeau, and Bernard Landry.

"It's a game of inches." A phrase often uttered by guys in Hamilton bars who not only have not heard of the referendum but also have never converted to the metric system.

"Fifty percent of winning is half mental." Preston Manning talking to a Francophone stop sign.

"That's below the belt." Where Preston Manning gets most of his brilliant ideas.

"They really came to play tonight." Definitely not the Quebec Nordiques, now known as the Colorado Fatal Snowslide.

"Our backs are against the wall." Defensive position practised by a non-white, non-French voter in a Quebec bar.

"He can play on my team any time." Buy-Me-a-Drink Boris Yeltsin offering Jacques Parizeau a Russian cabinet post. (Believing he'd been offered a Black Russian, Jacques accepted and announced his resignation as leader of the Parti Québécois.)

"A tie is like kissing your sister." In this case, that should read: "A tie is like French-kissing your sister." A disgusting thought to all guys, except a group of relatives living in Liverpool, Nova Scotia, where — how can I say this — everybody brings protection to the family reunions.

"It ain't over till the fat lady sings." This is a not so far-fetched scenario on how this whole constitution fiasco might end. Essentially, the Senate would have to ratify a new deal and yes, Pat Carney could cast the deciding vote.

If there's one hero to come out of the Quebec crisis, it would be the close aide to Jacques Parizeau, the one who said to him:

"Jacques, you're about to make the most important speech of your life, this speech could change the course of history, this speech . . .

Hey, buddy, let me freshen up that drink for you."

I believe there is one positive thing we can take away from this last referendum fiasco that would benefit all Canadian voters at all levels of government. Watching Jacques Parizeau at the microphone on referendum night, a little pissed and a lot pissed off, it occurred to me that what we need in order to get our political leaders to tell the truth is — the three-drink-minimum law.

Think about it. Any political person about to address Canadians from a political platform must knock back three hits of hard liquor before taking the stage. Then we'd get the truth. Then we'd get the speech that reads "My fellow Canadians, my friends, my loyal supporters, without you fine people blah, blah, blah" torn up and thrown in the air and then the bleary-eyed speaker would publicly, for the first time, give it to us straight.

"Why you snivelling little whiners — gimme, gimme, gimme — that's all I ever hear. My wife just left me, my kid's on crack, and last night the Mounties raided my law office. You think I care about the price of your prescription drugs? Here . . . (undoing his belt, dropping his pants, and bending over with his back to the audience) here's what I think about your petty little problems!" With that, the moon hits their eyes like a bigga pizza pie and that's *amore*.

Trust me, with the three-drink-minimum law, CHCH-TV will be cutting away from *Monday Night Football* to cover political speeches.

Surefire Signs Your Neighbours Are Russian Spies

W̶E LIVE IN TROUBLED TIMES HERE IN CANADA. SLIPPERY SLEUTHS, CROSS-eyed wire tappers, bribers, burglars, and dirty double-crossing secret agents — and that's just CSIS. Hey! They're on our side!

And that, of course, is the bad news. The good news is, apparently they caught some spies. Yes, the Canadian Security Intelligence Service (CSIS), which, like the Royal Canadian Mounted Police, is a wholly owned subsidiary of the Disney Corporation, actually flushed out and arrested a couple of Russian espionage agents. And you thought the only function of CSIS was to keep sending Grant Bristow change-of-address stickers.

Not so. Just the other day, a Toronto couple known as Laurie and Ian Lambert were arrested by Immigration Canada officers and accused of spying for Russia. In yet another mysterious incident, two ex-KGB operators were arrested north of Toronto on charges of arson and extortion.

It's frightening, bizarre, and downright dangerous. Just think, your own neighbours could be operating as foreign espionage agents. In case you're even a little bit suspicious, here's a few surefire signs that the couple living next door to you might be Russian spies.

• They have seven satellite dishes on their roof, but no television set in the house.

• The husband has pin-ups on the garage wall of fully dressed, overweight women know as *Pravda's* Sunshine Girls.

119

• Every time you talk politics with them, they ask if you mind being miked.

• After the husband flies his model airplane over your house, you see the wife running for the nearest photo shop with a roll of film in her hand.

• They're always bragging about how they supported the Nyet side in the referendum.

• Every Halloween they put hoods over their heads and go out as Igor Gouzenko.

• No matter who gets drunk and falls down at their parties, it's always Lenin who's under the glass coffee table.

• During the summer heat wave, they come to your door several times asking you to help them come in from the cold.

• Whenever you bump into the husband in a park he says, "Mary had a little lamb, her fleece was white as . . ." And when you say "snow," he hands you the secret blueprint for the Canadian Space Arm.

• They got noticeably agitated when you told them you'd cornered a mole in your back yard and killed it with a hoe.

• During Canada Day celebrations, the husband takes pictures of the parade with his digital watch.

• They line up for hours at the grocery store even if it's just them and the checkout lady.

• The first day the husband coached little league, he showed up with the equipment bag chained to his wrist.

• During the last election, they became confused when faced with more than one name on the ballot.

• When they come downstairs in the middle of the night, they're always relieved to find a burglar and not the police.

• They refuse to believe that the Canadian Navy just doesn't have any secrets!

• When a cop came to their door to warn them about break-ins in the area, they both swallowed their decoder rings.

• They buy front-row seats to every Detroit Red Wings home game and all they do is wink at Fetisov, Kozlov, Larionov, and Konstantinov.

Never mind the ghost stories you've been reading to your kids. If CSIS is right about this being just the tip of the iceberg, those could be real spooks looking in your windows.

The Classic Canadian Criminal Mind: Missing in Action

TODAY WE WILL TAKE A CRITICAL LOOK INTO THE COMMON CANADIAN criminal mind hoping to find . . . Whoa! There's enough room in here to park a Zamboni and host a peewee hockey tournament! And dark too!

Governments in Canada at all levels are on a cost-cutting crusade. Vowing to save us from an avalanche of debt, our leaders are diligently and systematically removing people from social assistance programs and transferring them over to the department of crime. Apparently, the words of safe cracker Willy Sutton have not yet sunk into the brains of the financial geniuses wrestling with our fiscal fiasco. When asked why he robbed banks, Willy said quite simply: "Because that's where the money is."

Banks in Canada have all the money. The big four skimmed a billion each in pure profit last year. Banks in Canada are the same institutions holding those IOUs over our heads and escalating federal and provincial debt with obscene interest rates. Yet banks in Canada wouldn't lend you a dime without first holding a quarter in collateral. The solution is simple. Banks in Canada need to be robbed, legal-like. Send in the Mounties, burn all the loan agreements, transfer all the money to Ottawa and the provincial capitals, and start over. Do it on a Monday, a bank holiday.

Thanks for listening.

Meanwhile, back on Planet Earth, you've just been a victim of cost-cutting and you're about to take that first big step into the world

of crime. Be smart. Learn from the experience of criminals now practising in this country.

For example, in Vernon, B.C., recently, a bandit walked into a pharmacy and told the employee that he would be back in thirty minutes to rob the place. RCMP who arrested the man and his accomplice confirmed that the robber was not only good on his word but also punctual.

Question: Is crime so prevalent in this country that you are now required to make a reservation?

Answer: No. Although it's always best to rob an establishment during non-peak periods, reservations are not recommended. And yes, the old "element of surprise" technique still has a certain amount of charm to it.

In Coldwater, Ontario, burglars put a tad too much firepower in the night deposit box when they robbed the Toronto-Dominion Bank. Most of the cash burned up and the blast woke up the neighbours, who flocked to the scene and scooped up those bills that survived the fire.

Question: How much is too much TNT?

Answer: It's a judgment call.

Better question: How can I discourage pajama-clad non-members of my gang from joining in the robbery?

Answer: It's always a good idea to rob banks in upscale neighbourhoods where residents are too involved in white-collar and computer crime to come down to the street in their pajamas.

In Peterborough, Ontario, a suspected criminal named Anthony Duco gave an alias to the police who were questioning him. Unfortunately, the name he gave police was that of his own brother. Most unfortunately, his brother was wanted on a sexual assault charge. Police got two Ducos for the price of one.

Question: When preparing an alias, a pseudonym, or even a false passport, is it best to go outside your immediate family in selecting a name?

Answer: Always. In fact, many professional criminals select names from newspaper obituary columns, being careful to avoid those periods preceded by an untimely death in the family.

A man who robbed a retail outlet in Kingston, Ontario, was caught because while out on bail the very next day he went back and robbed the same store. The name of the store — I'm not making this up — was Déjà Vu.

Question: What's Déjà Vu and is there some kind of grace period that criminals respect in regards to frequency of visitation to the same job site?

Answer: Déjà Vu was a promising young Vietnamese artist who studied under Picasso and died from all that weight on his chest. When it comes to repeat same-place robbery, four is too few for department stores, two is too many for street vendors. When in doubt, spread yourself around a bit.

In Kitchener, Ontario, Phil Armstrong was charged with robbing a sub shop with a bullet. Not a gun, but a bullet.

Question: What kind of threat did Phil make to the staff?

Answer: Phil said, and I quote: "Gimme all the money and a large Italian salami to go or I'll bite down on this here bullet and gravely wound you all with flying molar shrapnel!"

(Writer's note: Common criminal weapon selection is so important, I have devoted an entire chapter to it. Please see: "Throw Down Your Can Opener and Come Out with Your Hands Up!")

In downtown Toronto, a man robbed a Mac's Milk store with an eight-inch knife while wearing his underwear over his head as a disguise.

Question: Boxers or briefs?

Answer: While the centre fly in a pair of boxer shorts allows the robber's nose to stick out for better breathing, the more angular and curved fly in a pair of briefs, when worn upside down, can provide some peripheral visibility for the right eye. Depending upon how long you've been wearing your underwear, good air may take precedence over sight lines. Please remember to back out of the store: certain stains could become a trademark. Nobody, not even the lowliest of criminals, deserves the nickname "Skid."

In Port Colborne, Ontario, three men were arrested after a record-setting spree of robbing six Toronto banks in one day. The previous record was five in one day.

Question: Fame or fortune?

Answer: If you focus on the fortune now, the fame will inevitably come later. Like sex, quantity over quality is a mistake often made by amateurs. You rob a bank for the money. Period. Getting your name in the record books is something a consummate professional will try to avoid.

In Vineland, Ontario, a man who robbed the local credit union slipped while hastily leaving the scene in his van and fell out the driver's door, running himself over with his own getaway vehicle. True.

Question: As a one-person operation just starting out, is it risky to try to do everything yourself?

Answer: Yes. Statistics Canada will verify that stress in this country is the greatest killer of new single proprietorship businesses. This is followed closely by insufficient capital and snow tire tracks on the inner thigh. There are plenty of federal training programs that allow you to hire part-time help in the areas of transportation, planning, and accounting.

I sincerely hope by reviewing these case studies, your life in crime will not be spent mostly in cuffs and leg irons.

I trust you'll understand that putting the common Canadian criminal mind under a microscope, as I have done here, is the only way you get to see anything at all.

Question: What seems to be the driving force behind today's typical Canadian crook?

Answer: Nothing that regular doses of Beano can't cure.

Yard Sale People: Bond 'Em

THIS STORY COULD BE A MAJOR COUNTRY AND WESTERN SONG COMING soon to a jukebox near you: "Yard sale people got no class. Yard sale people even spit on my grass. Got more junk than when I set up my table. Yard sale people are quirky and unstable." (Okay, so it doesn't have the insightful subtleties of "Achy Breaky Heart," but you get the picture.)

In my opinion, yard sale people, all yard sale people — sellers, buyers, lookers, and brokers — should be bonded and fitted with electronic ankle bracelets so we know where they are every minute of the day. A beeper should go off when we come within pickpocket proximity of each other.

The traditional Canadian yard/lawn/garage sale is actually an outdoor insult contest in which pieces of junk and spare change are the agreed-upon weapons of choice.

Take me, for instance, your principal peddler for today's yard seller. With a card table, a jar of change, and no experience whatsoever, I will take a decade's worth of accumulated junk, which I'm too embarrassed to drop off at the local dump, and I will attempt to sell it to you, an unsuspecting stranger. By the time we meet in my driveway, I will have gone through these five strategies of yard sale marketing:

1. I don't care if I make any money as long as I get rid of this crap.

2. Hey! These still work.

3. I don't think five bucks is too much. I probably paid ten.

4. If they don't want to pay full price, I'll just keep 'em and use 'em myself.

5. Write tags like "Plastic salt & pepper shakers $15 once used by Elvis."

So that's me, the seller, sitting casually in a lawn chair with a cup of coffee and the morning paper, appearing nonchalant and above all this neighbourhood nonsense. I know what evil lurks behind those masking-tape price stickers. I am a swindler.

Now let's take you. You are the prospective yard sale customer, a buyer that ought to be very wary. You are my market, my mark. First of all, you arrived at 7:30 A.M. when the ads specified "9:00 A.M. start." You knocked on my door and shouted something about a sale. I shouted back something about your mama. (Sorry.)

You returned later, parked in my neighbour's flower garden, and after inspecting every item in the yard sale, you picked up my card table with my entire sale inventory, empty coffee mug, and newspaper and said: "Would you take a quarter for this?"

As politely as I could, I said, "No, but for fifty cents you could get that canoe paddle . . . right across your back!" (Again, I apologize.)

So as a professional yard sale customer, you're rude, cold-hearted, and crass. Yard sale people are a pain in the ass. You're the reason K-Mart won't hire a sales staff. But that's your job. You're supposed to make me feel cheap and sleazy. After all, I'm a swindler. If I didn't want to be humiliated I wouldn't have taken out ads in the newspaper inviting you to come to my house and fondle my personal belongings. You're the type of person whose children will grow up to be scalpers, mine will supply them with counterfeit concert tickets.

It's a very sick world. I'm just glad we could be there for each other. And who gains from a yard sale? Bob.

Bob is my neighbour, and until our five-family yard sale last weekend, a relatively sane human being. Tragically, Bob was stricken by the deadly yard sale virus early that Saturday morning.

This otherwise shy and quiet man began screaming at and chasing cars on Lakeshore Road until, fearing for their lives, the drivers pulled into vacant fields, where Bob pushed yard sale merchandise through open windows, and when the people realized he was not going to physically harm them, they gave him money. With this unique sales technique, Bob sold all of his stuff and a lot of mine.

We managed to stop Bob only seconds before he completed a

handshake deal that involved his two sons, a sit-down mower, and $75 dollars in cash.

So what do we learn from all this?

Well, the old adage about human nature and material value is as true today as it ever was: "One man's junk is another man's junk."

Yard sale people. Bond 'em and bind 'em at the ankles electronically.

Modern Inventions;
Alexander Graham Bell,
Please Phone Home

As a concerned citizen of this planet, which is rapidly running out of food, fresh water, and clean air while doubling its population every couple of years, you will be pleased to know that right now industrious inventors are hard at work and spending billions of dollars to create products that will enhance your life. Products like the Hay Fever Hat.

The Hay Fever Hat is a roll of toilet paper attached to a chin strap so you can wear it on your head, as close as possible to the sources of coughing and sneezing. I should warn you that wearing the Hay Fever Hat while driving a car can be hazardous, unless you tuck the end of the roll in your ear. This is a cost-cutting measure designed to eliminate the need for a Q-Tip.

(Warning: Those wrapping the end of the roll around their heads could wind up being hired by the RCMP.)

Other merchandising miracles you'll find on the modern marketplace are the Eye Drop Funnel Glasses, which allow you to hit an eye drop bull's-eye every time; the Bath Body Suit, plastic coveralls that allow you to experience the warmth of a bath without getting wet; and Detachable Tooth Covers, plastic gum inserts that keep your teeth clean while you eat.

Not only will all three items confirm your life-long worship of polyester, they also create a swell Halloween ensemble.

Last year, Duster Slippers for Cats, footwear designed to collect dust while your cat walked around the house, didn't prove too successful. Half the cats outfitted with the oversized socks were too damn lazy to get off the couch and the other half frantically ran around trying to dislodge the footwear, smashing things along the way.

Undaunted, this year the same creators now bring you Daddy Nurser, a pair of artificial breasts with shoulder straps that enable fathers to experience the joy of breast-feeding. (Guys, please remember to remove your breasts before heading off to the poker game.)

In Vancouver, for $12, you can take your mutt to Launderdog, a self-service shampoo pit stop complete with soap, brushes, towels, and dryers. (Pass on the hot wax.)

At the Park Bench Café in Huntington Beach, California, your dog can sit next to you at the table and order off the all-new dog menu. A plate of five dog biscuits will run him fifty cents; the Wrangler Roundup (a ground turkey patty) is $2.25. The big bonus here is that if you get worked over by a surly waiter, the dog can register your displeasure by running up and biting the guy on the ass.

In Japan, inventor Yoshiro Nakamatsu has come up with Yummi Nutri Brain Biscuits. He claims they boost your pet's IQ. Apparently they taste just like the Park Bench Café's dog biscuits. The difference is after the dog fetches the morning paper for you, he'll also read you the sports.

The inventor claims that his brain foods, when taken in conjunction with his exercise and sex creations, can extend your life to the age of 144 years. His exercise and sex inventions are — I hope you're sitting down — spring-loaded jogging shoes and the Love-Jet clitoral stimulator. (Do not, I repeat, do not operate these pieces of equipment at the same time. And that certainly applies to men who are breast-feeding!)

But the product that I think best displays the spirit of entrepreneurship in the 1990s is olestra, Procter and Gamble's zero-calorie fake-fat cooking oil developed at the cost of $25 million (U.S.). A typical serving of potato chips contains 10 grams of fat and 150 calories. Made with olestra, the same serving has zero fat and just 60 calories.

The U.S. Food and Drug Administration has approved the use of olestra even though it causes stomach cramps, diarrhea, and flatulence.

(And if you think you're surprised, you should see the looks on the faces of the Fruit of the Loom boys!) Olestra passes through the body too fast to clog arteries or create fat. Just imagine edible WD-40 coursing through your digestive track so fast it sets off the body's photo radar cameras and then mysteriously disappears at the end of the line with a bang. Procter and Gamble plans to introduce olestra in its Pringles potato chips. The new slogan: "Eat 'em, get set, go!"

Fast-food customer: "Gimme a double order of olestra fries and clear those kids outta that hallway — I'm going to eat 'em here."

You may think spending $25 million (U.S.) so we can enjoy fat-free potato chips is a frivolous waste of money. I disagree. I see olestra as a major scientific breakthrough and a real job booster, since its side effects will dramatically increase the sales of that Hay Fever Hat.

And in the spirit of '90s inventiveness, the world of modern medicine — "parts is parts" — brings you human McNuggets.

I watch a lot of news on television and read two newspapers a day, and few things ever surprise me. Last month I was sitting in my room at the Senator Hotel in Timmins, Ontario, whose community slogan is: "Hey! If you think this is cold, don't ever play Fetch the Flag naked in February in Geraldton." I was watching NBC news when I was startled by a mouse, this hairless, pink little laboratory rodent, carrying a human ear on its back. I am not making this up.

The next day, when I was finally able to close my mouth and walk, I got a morning paper, which told the rest of the story complete with a photo.

The mouse, carrying the human ear like a knapsack, is the result of a successful chemical-engineering experiment at the Massachusetts Institute of Technology in which human body parts are being "grown" by animals. Now, instead of replacing damaged or lost human parts with artificial substitutes, scientists can implant your living cells under the skin of an animal, insert a form around which the cells will grow, and the animal supplies the nourishment to naturally create an ear, a nose, a liver, bones, even teeth that are yours, DNA-lly speaking.

Thank goodness this breakthrough in organ reproduction happened now and not two years earlier. Instead of reattachment, John Wayne Bobbitt may have opted for this new regeneration process and we'd be witnessing the first-ever work stoppage by laboratory mice.

First mouse: "Oh, no, not a chance. There ain't enough cheese in Wisconsin to get me to carry that thing around on my back."

Second mouse: "Don't look at me. With my luck, that crazy woman will break into the lab and cut if off a second time. Forget it."

The M.I.T. article quoted the bioengineering department head as saying, "Tissue engineering will forever change the medical landscape."

I have no doubts. It's already changed the way I eat supper in front of the television set.

Today regrowing your own body parts is a medical miracle, tomorrow it'll be as common as laser surgery. First there will be a huge demand, followed by an even bigger supply and then . . . advertising! No doubt the manufacturing of body parts will flourish first in the United States, the land of loaded guns and killer knives, where people seem to be losing a lot of vital organs at an ever-increasing rate. I can see it now: billboards right across the country. An earless Van Gogh eyes a mouse with the human ear on its back and says: "Friends, rodents, countrymen, lend me that freakin' ear!" Underneath the trademark: "M.I.T. — we're listening."

The competition to furnish parts will be fierce.

"Don't have a leg to stand on? You do now. Send two tissue cells and $49.99 (plus shipping and handling) to Gams To Go, Box 838, New York, NY. (Please note: previous problems with those pranksters at the post office have been eliminated. Your new legs will now be delivered in proper packaging, instead of just walking up and kicking your door. Management apologizes for any inconvenience in the past.)"

"Get off on the wrong foot today? Put your foot in it, did you? Got one foot in the grave? No problem. Call Fleet Feet, 1-800-TEN-TOES. And remember, if we can't deliver a new pair of feet to you within two hours, your next pair of ankles are free!"

"Despise sobriety? Detest detox? Well, get your sorry butt down here to Livers While-U-Wait. That's right. Relax at our on-premises shooters bar while a pig of your own choice grows a new liver for you. Bring the kids and feed the animals at our Vital Organ Petting Zoo. Remember our guarantee: either that little porker produces you a liver, or he's a year's supply of back bacon."

Of all the organs medical science will reproduce in the future, the human brain would seem to be the one man needs the most.

And they're getting closer than you think. Scientists at the University of California have actually synthesized pantetheine, thereby recreating the primordial slime from which all life forms evolved on this planet, including you and me. Scientists call this the soup of life. I prefer to call it "human noodle," but that may not mean much to you because you've never met my brother-in-law.

Scientists are now knocking down the natural boundaries between species faster than a tomato can scream, "Feed me, stupid!"

I'm not kidding. British Columbian scientists recently revealed a study in which tomato plants deprived of water and wired with tiny microphones emit audible sounds of stress. This would explain an incident at A&P the other day when I squeezed an overripe Italian plum tomato, causing juice to spurt out, and I distinctly heard it call me a *pazzo*.

The purpose of the B.C. study was to get plants to utter an audible signal that would trigger water systems so, unsupervised, they could one day shower themselves. If it works, they plan to try it on teenagers.

In another experiment, scientists have successfully transplanted the genes of a firefly into a tobacco plant, causing it to glow at night. This is true. Fireflies always did light up after sex; now they get to smoke too.

Believe me, in the realm of modern medicine, it won't be long before a Frankenstein rookie card is worth $5,000.

Scientists used to create things like insulin, radar, nylon — useful things that nudged the human condition to a higher level. Last week, they revealed their latest prize: a foreskin the size of six soccer fields. Honest. This kind of thing leaves a man feeling woefully inadequate and hoping with all his heart that he never has to share a jail cell with the guy at the other end of it. In fairness, this gigantic sheet of tissue manufactured from the skin of one circumcised baby may someday save the lives of burn victims and transplant patients. But I'm warning you — if it ever gets out of — sorry, if it ever escapes from the lab, the world doesn't make a condom large enough to capture this thing.

Exasperated lab scientist: "Sid, it's no use. It just flinched and wiped out Louisville. We gotta send in Lorena!"

Almost all of this scientific abracadabra is tolerable, but the one that stopped me in my tracks was the recent experiment by Swiss scientists that produced fruit flies with eyes on their antennae, wings, and legs. Honest. One fruit fly came out of the experiment with fourteen fully developed eyes. Unfortunately, with the diversity of that many eyes, the fruit fly's strength of vision was weakened, and they're now fitting him for seven pairs of prescription sunglasses.

The other problem is, he hasn't been able to fly since his right leg and left wing got into a staring contest.

There was no real purpose to this experiment. It was just a slow day in the lab and a bunch of guys named Rudi and Gerhart decided to have fun with fruit flies.

It's very scary. Be careful. The next time you get a little irritated and say, "Hey, whaddayathink — I got eyes in the back of my head?" you may have just placed an order.

It's official: at the midway point of this decade, necessity is no longer the mother of invention. I believe Weird Al Yankovich is now the mother of invention.

Up! Up! And Away Up to Our Knees in Cow Poop

Every once in a while, I like to do something extremely dangerous, and since nobody in their right mind wants to die alone, I always bring my brother-in-law Danny along. Danny is very different from me in that he hates doing dangerous things. But Danny can be tricked.

"You wanna go to the States, Dan, and drink champagne in a field?" I asked.

"Okay, Bill," he replied. "What do I wear?"

A few hours later, near Mayville, New York, we stopped in the parking lot of the Good Morning Farm to watch a group of locals assembling one of those gigantic hot air balloons. We left the car to get a closer look and soon enough we were tugging and untangling ropes, unfolding and separating pleats of nylon.

Standing beside the small wooden basket as they inflated the balloon, we were rapidly dwarfed by it — a 90,000 cubic foot teardrop of nylon bursting with the fiery heat of two propane jets and measuring seven stories high at its fullness.

"Okay," said Captain John. "Get in, Dan."

"How'd he know my name, Bill?" asked Danny.

"He's a psychic balloonist, Dan. He knows everybody's name," I said. "He used to work with a crystal ball and all his clients said he was full of hot air and so one day . . ."

"I'll get you for this, Bill," said Danny as several crew members stuffed him into the basket. At this point, I tried to cut and run, thinking it would be great to be an interested spectator at a dangerous event, but they hauled me in too.

Danny, who has a deep-seated fear of heights, didn't want to go. If I learned one thing from three years at an accredited Canadian university, it's the art of subtle persuasion. So I tucked my thumbs in my armpits and began flailing my arms up and down, all the while circling Danny and making a clucking noise. The crew managed to remove Danny's hands from my throat just in time for take-off.

From that moment on, it was, as the song says, some kind of wonderful. You rise, slowly, effortlessly, as if by spirit. The countryside slowly shrinks below your feet. Everything on earth gets smaller and quieter until it reflects a shade of serenity you can only wish it possessed.

There is no noise or wind resistance because you are the wind, drifting oddly on unseen natural currents over landscape you've never seen from this implausible perspective. And you float: just above the treetops, just beneath the clouds. You sweep across a sunburst horizon, gazing down at this still-life fresco of farms and villages frozen by distance. It's like dying and slowly ascending into heaven, except you realize you're with your brother-in-law, so technically that would be impossible.

And the real neat part? It drives dogs nuts. The occasional blast of the propane burners that propel us makes a sound that startles animals on the ground, made worse by the fact that it's coming from somewhere over their heads. Inside of thirty minutes, we had every dog in Chautauqua County howling and yapping and running in circles. As a postie, Danny didn't find this quite as amusing as I did.

It was as peaceful and reverent an experience as I've ever had. Right up until we hit the tree.

Trees, as Danny was quick to point out to me, are the natural enemy of airborne balloons. If you accept the idea that a balloon is a ship on a sea of sky, trees are kind of like icebergs.

By law, Captain John, our friendly flight commander, had to bring the balloon down by sunset. The prevailing currents of wind had brought us over forests and houses, we spooked deer and we stopped traffic, but now that you needed one, there was nary an open field to be found. John tried an abrupt and awkward landing in an open corner of a roadside field, and we would have made it too if a rope hadn't got tangled in a branch of that tree and our basket came hard into the upper limbs.

That's when Danny said the bad word: "Holy ——— ."

Did I mention people on the ground, of which there were several dozen, can hear a pin drop on the floor of the balloon's basket? Yeah, well, there's a minister in Chautauqua who still can't figure out how the thing Danny mentioned could be interpreted as a blessed event.

I got the crowd back on our side, however, when, in a valiant effort to rid the balloon of ballast, I tried to throw my brother-in-law overboard.

But Captain John saved the day when he so skillfully and smoothly brought that balloon in for a beautiful humorous landing. Actually, that should read humus landing.

He claimed he didn't know that the Wellman farm was completely carpeted by a foot and a half of the richest, ripest, squishiest cow manure in all the county.

But he was still laughing when he pulled away with the crew van, leaving Danny and me wading around up to our knees, groping for our footwear.

And yes, we did drink champagne in a field. In ballooning, it's a tradition.

Damn, but I love it when a plan comes together.

Adam Beck Is Not a Sissy! Is Not! Is Not!

LAST NIGHT I PASSED UP KARAOKE NIGHT AT THE BELMONT HOTEL WHERE the feature act was fifteen ladies from the bingo hall next door line-dancing and lip-synching the words to "Get Your Tongue Out of My Mouth, I'm Kissing You Good-bye."

Instead, I attended the Port Colborne premier of *Job and the Snake*, a contemporary rock musical much like *Hair*, except all the actors kept their clothes on because their parents were in the audience.

It's a very good stage play, richly enhanced by the role of Job, but somewhat lacking in a snake. I think the snake referred to in the title is the biblical symbol for Satan, but I'm not sure because I went to see the play before reading the book.

It's a classic struggle between good and evil in which good triumphs in the end by driving Satan out of Job's life using loud electronically enhanced music in much the same way the U.S. Marines drove Manuel Noriega out of the Catholic safe house in Panama a few years ago.

As I said, it's a good play, but it has one serious fault. Early in the first act, the hapless but innocent Job loses everything — his possessions, his wife, his children — and for the rest of that scene, a confused audience is left waiting for the appearance of the wife's lawyer. Hey, I'm kidding. There were no lawyers in the Bible, which is why we still refer to it as the book of miracles. (There were a few asps with attitudes, but that was it.)

I must admit I wasn't paying much attention to the play. I was focussing on the acting debut of Adam Beck, my neighbour's son and my main supplier of cheese and other door-to-door fundraising products from Wainfleet South Public School. (Motto: We Bring K-Mart into Your Kitchen Whether You Like It or Not.) Adam appeared on stage in a very cool but unbiblical flannel shirt, dancing and swooning in the "Serpent Song," as well as the "Curse God and Die" sequence.

Few were aware that Adam Beck (Sir, to his friends) did not want to be up on that stage. You see, the Sherk boys had told Adam that it would be kind of wussy to sing and dance with a bunch of girls, even if it would help reinforce Job's unshakable faith in God. So, Adam naturally declined the key role of Job's son, the name of whom escaped Adam when I interviewed him several times for this story.

Enter stage left, John Beck, Adam's real-life father, who, unlike Job, being not above sin, bribed Adam to take the role. The deal was if Adam stayed in the play for its Port Colborne run, he would inherit his older brother Jamie's BB gun.

You see, I alone knew this piece of crucial information. The audience was completely unaware of the inner conflict churning, churning, churning in the guts of Job's son (name still not available).

Even Adam's real-life mother, Jan, was oblivious to this unholy inner conflict tormenting her son, because I could clearly see she was still on speaking terms with John.

Knowing more about the character's situation than the actors and the audience, I was in a position of detached superiority and hence able to foresee the outcome, contrary to everyone else's expectation. This is known as dramatic irony.

The outcome that I foresaw was the Sherk boys spilling the beans, their mother calling Adam's mother, and John sleeping on my couch for a week or so. This is known as tragic irony.

Adam Beck's inner conflict between dancing for the unfailing trust in the Lord and getting his mitts on that BB gun came to a head just after the "I Am Not a Rock" score.

While every other actor was chanting "You get no shame when you got no blame," Adam was delivering his own silent soliloquy: "Divine justice? Do not speak to me of divine justice! Because if I possesseth that Daisy BB gun whilst I swoon and dance, I'd pumpeth off two quick shots into yonder butt of the evil Satan and we could all go home early and happy. Restoration of faith and reputation? Huh? When those despairing loutish Sherk fellows see me with my trusty Daisy, then they shall feel for all eternity the awful ache of jealousy." (It sounded a lot better when Sir Adam was silently saying it.)

A splendid performance was delivered by Adam Beck, flawless in technique, until he accidentally collided with his sister Kelly in "The Spirit Is Movin'" number.

Adam is not a sissy. He's a man, long suffering the hardship of the paradoxical human conscience. I say to you with complete confidence that Adam Beck is a real man, except shorter. Dance on ye young (name still not available at press time), dance on!

The play ended prematurely when, with everybody on stage dancing around the deflated Prince of Darkness, pointing accusatory fingers, making hate gestures, and delivering mortal curses, a man in the back of the theatre, unable to take it any more, stood up and shouted: "Hey, it's not Bob Rae, for godsakes. It's only Satan. Ease up, eh?"

Churches; They're Not Just for Religion Any More

As America deals with the dreadful dilemma that some of the worst enemies of the states are in fact *from* the States, it's interesting to look back at Waco.

The first question I had upon learning about the Branch Davidian cult in Texas was, how difficult is it for a guy to start his own church and religion?

I attended a somewhat religious school, Waterloo Lutheran University, but they encouraged us to start our own business.

At the graduation ceremony, nobody looked at me and said: "The robes look great on you, buddy, now get out there and play God."

Can anybody just become head of a church — no training, no certification, no manual?

Apparently, David Koresh did, and I imagine it must have happened like this:

"I'd like to thank you all for coming this afternoon. My name is Vernon Howell, but you could call me David, Messiah of God and King of the Hebrews. Now about this church thing, I'll be Jesus Christ and the rest of you —-

"What? I know it was only a minute ago I was David, Messiah of God and King of the Hebrews, but now I'm Jesus, all right. This is a fast-track creation, man. We don't need no committees. We don't have like centuries and centuries to get this thing up and running, okay?

"So, as I said, I'll be Jesus, you guys in the back there, you'll all be my disciples and — what? Disciples, you know, like teachers and followers. Like, I'll give you the word and you guys go forth and spread it. Just don't spread it too thin, okay? Look, I've only been God for what, like, five minutes, man, so I don't have all the answers. You guys

142

are going to have to figure some of this stuff out for yourselves.

"This is like improv divinity, man. Get with the program, okay?

"So as I was saying, I'll be Jesus, all you guys are my disciples, and since you're going to be busy spreading my word and stuff, I'll sleep with your wives. All in favour? Great. Thank you for your support and throw some cash in the plate on your way out.

"Oh, and Matt, you and Luke take the truck to town. Let's see, we need some peanut butter, a gallon of lamb's blood, and enough semi-automatic weapons to fight off the FBI for approximately two years. And, Matt, get the latest Grateful Dead tape and a bag of that candy that crackles and fizzes in your mouth . . . Yeah, Hot Rocks."

Is this pretty much how this thing in Waco, Texas, got started?

Not being a religious person, there was a lot of this David Koresh and the Branch Davidian thing I just did not understand. At all the meetings of all the minds of all major religions, did nobody think to lay down a few ground rules for starting up a church?

Simple things like giving God a jersey with #1 on the back and once he retires, nobody else can ever wear that number again.

Common-sense stuff, like anybody who has a big nose and glasses and is kind of dorky looking probably isn't God. He's probably just some loon named Vernon.

Some limitations, like no church can stockpile more offensive combat weapons than a country the size of Nicaragua.

I don't know about you, but I think I'd be a little nervous attending a church where the leader has an arsenal of AK-47s, M-16s, 9-mm pistols, and a .50-calibre machine gun. You can be sure of one thing, however. In a well-armed church, nobody fiddles with the money on the collection plate.

What do you say when you're sitting in the confessional and you begin with "Forgive me, Father, for I have sinned" and the person on the other side of that little window fires a warning shot over your head? I tell you what you say — *everything!* Boy, make stuff up if you have to! Tell him everything he wants to hear.

I remember watching a television interview with David Koresh's grandmother, who rambled on in defence of the Branch Davidian leader, quoting Scriptures and confirming once and for all that mental illness is mostly genetic. She ended by saying: "He's just a man who needs to be loved."

I thought to myself, the man has nineteen wives, lady; it's not as if he isn't trying!

If there's any question about David Koresh's sanity, let's remember that he married one woman about his own age and then he married her mother. Now I ask you, would you believe divine revelations as explained to you by a guy who married his own mother-in-law? I don't think so.

If I were to start a church it would harmonize the spiritual forces at work in the world, like Yin, the passive principle of Chinese philosophy at once being enhanced by and in balance with Yang, a reputable Hong Kong silk shirtmaker. That would be the basis of my religion — laid back and comfortably dressed.

I'm sorry, but I don't think I'm cut out for a cult. I could never be a David Koresh. I can't imagine stopping at the Belmont Hotel for a few beers and having to phone home nineteen times to explain why I'm going to be a little late for supper.

In Canada We Hijack Buses

(APRIL 1996 MARKED THE SEVENTH ANNIVERSARY OF CANADA'S
VERY FIRST DOMESTIC TERRORIST INCIDENT
AND THIS REPORT OF THE EVENT.)

FRANKLY, FOLKS, IF WE CAN'T PRODUCE A BETTER BRAND OF TERRORIST AND anti-terrorist in this country, we are a nation doomed.

Take the recent hijacking of Greyhound Bus no. 1482. Take it and turn it into a comedy starring Danny DeVito as the terrorist, John Candy as the bus driver, and the cast of *Police Academy VIII* as everybody else.

First up, a Canadian of Lebanese origin sets out from Montreal with a handgun to create a hostage-taking incident, thus drawing attention to the plight of Christians in his homeland.

Nothing wrong with this, it happens every afternoon in the best European and Arab countries. But here in Canada, our very first hijacker, what does the guy do? He hijacks a bus. This was a big mistake.

I looked it up in *The Hijackers' Handbook* and it clearly states in chapter 1 under "Vehicle Selection": "In the final analysis, forcibly commandeering any vehicle incapable of flight is really !@#%*! impractical" — not to mention nationally humiliating when a bus driver falls out of his seat in a fit of laughter after you order him: "Fly this baby to Beirut!" Any student of physics, even a failing student of physics, will tell you pigs will fly before buses.

Further down the page, golfcarts, bulldozers, dirt bikes, and the Ford Pinto are listed as other examples of poor vehicle selection.

Nonetheless, our hijacker, our very own Canadian hijacker, has his gun drawn and his Greyhound in high gear when he faces his first real test: a passenger — of which there were eleven on this bus destined for New York City — objects to the hijacker's erratic behaviour.

So what does our hijacker do? He kicks this guy off the bus. This was a big mistake.

Once again I consulted *The Hijackers' Handbook,* under "Hostage Resistance," and I quote: "In the event of a hostage attempting to object, impede or in any way obstruct your terrorist operation once it is under way — shoot the sucker!"

Can you see this working with the American and European hostages they're holding in Beirut right now? This swarthy terrorist has them all chained to this filthy hovel in Beirut and he's pacing back and forth with his Uzi submachine gun and a hostage in the back puts up his hand and the terrorist says, "What's your problem?"

And the hostage says, "I don't like the food here," and the terrorist says, "Oh, yeah, well then you can just get the hell out of here, buddy!" And he throws the guy out onto the street.

I suppose the problem was not that our hijacker released this man, it's that he forgot to threaten him at gunpoint with: "And you better not tell anybody about this neither!"

Subsequently, the passenger, a born spoilsport, walked to an emergency phone and told everybody about the hijacking. Of course he's a little steamed, he'd purchased a round-trip ticket, for goodness sakes.

Normally, with the proper authorities alerted, this could have meant the end of the escapade. Almost anywhere but Canada. But not here, not in this case, because the released hostage didn't contact real police, he contacted the Quebec Provincial Police.

When they learned of the hijacked bus, they assumed nobody, not even a crazed terrorist, would want to take a bus trip across Canada in April, so believing he was headed south, they contacted the police in Vermont and nobody else.

This was a big mistake. Because now we have no police looking for the hijacked bus in Canada, but we do have a sheriff in Vermont, unfamiliar with the term "Greyhound Bus Lines," looking for a crazed and armed Canadian riding a skinny dog south down Interstate 91.

Meanwhile, on board the New York–bound bus, the hijacker, as a way of explaining his actions, recounted stories to his hostages about the killings, the car bombings, and the homeless people living in the streets of Beirut.

Appreciative of a man baring his soul with tales of anguish and despair, the hostages ached to share something with their captor. So they told him stories about the killings, the car bombings, and the homeless people living in the streets of New York City.

To which the hijacker (remember, we're dealing with a man who is only allegedly nuts, not stupid) told the driver: "Drive this bus to Ottawa. Nothing ever happens there!"

Two hours later the bus showed up at the House of Commons, which, by my calculations, improves Greyhound's arrival time for the Montreal-to-Ottawa run by a full fifteen minutes.

But things were not going well for our hijacker. During the two-hour trip nobody chased the bus or tried to force it off the road. I mean, who knew? Once on Parliament Hill, nobody stopped him, nobody noticed, nobody cared. Welcome to federal government.

So they pull onto Parliament Hill in the middle of the afternoon and our government is in session, which means the lights are on, the bells are ringing, and everybody's asleep in chambers.

The first thing that happens is a tour bus cuts off the hijacked bus and takes his parking spot. The hijacker gets into a shouting match with the tour-bus driver, but the guy claimed he got there first and he's not budging.

Well, as an armed terrorist with a troop of hostages, the last thing you expect to be confronted by is rudeness. "I don't care about a home-land for the Palestinians, that's my bloody parking spot!"

So the hijacker orders his bus driver to take the vehicle onto the lawn of Parliament Hill, where it sinks in soft grass up to its axles. That's pretty much the end of the chase scene right there.

Little consolation to the terrorist, but the bus is just one more thing, not the first nor the last, to wind up in the sink hole known as Ottawa.

Then our hijacker sends one of the hostages out with a terrorist note listing all his demands, and — you guessed it — nobody can read the guy's handwriting. Meanwhile on the bus, the hostages by their own admission were, and I quote, "telling jokes and stories and exchanging family photos from their wallets."

Boy, here's a group of people who'll be having flashbacks and nightmares for the rest of their lives, eh?

Now the hijacker is so frustrated he walks down the steps of the bus, opens the door, and fires two shots into the lawn.

Well, obviously our hijacker knows nothing about Canada, because nobody shoots a lawn in Ottawa and gets away with it! The Mounties swarmed the place — weapons bigger than the officers carrying them, sirens wailing, emergency tactical vehicles, the bomb squad — nobody in that town could remember such an all-out police assault since two joints of marijuana were found in Margaret Trudeau's fridge.

All this happened outside Prime Minister Mulroney's office and he was absolutely unaware of it until he got into his limo headed for the airport and an aide warned him on his car phone of a sniper.

Sniper? Apparently, the riddled bodies of four blades of grass had been discovered by this time.

Here's a man who claims to be on top of the fast-changing events in China, but he doesn't know about a hijacking taking place under his office window. I love a leader with vision.

And by the way, with Prime Minister Mulroney, Joe Clark, John Crosbie — all the big boys — in Ottawa that day, did you notice the hijacker made no attempt to take one of them hostage? No sir, he knows!

He knows if he takes one of our top politicians hostage what he's going to get from the Canadian people: SUPPORT! Unquestioned support! Along with food, blankets, plane tickets. Whaddayaneed? Whendayaneedit?

Eventually, however, our hijacker just gave up in disgust. If the police didn't care enough to report him or chase him, if the hostages were just going to sit around chatting and exchanging family photos and planning the first annual hostage reunion, if the prime minister was going to drive by and practically wave at him, then to hell with it. Why bother?

Looking back on this whole operation, you have to be relieved that our hijacker didn't burn himself on the Eternal Flame over on nearby Wellington Street.

The man simply quit. It's just my hunch, but I think the flap over the parking spot demoralized him the most.

Advice to the next would-be Canadian terrorist? You're up against one of the greatest national police forces in the world. Practise penmanship and bring a parking pass.

I hope Canada is proud of itself. In typical Canadian fashion, mediocrity and indifference have yet again succeeded in killing the spirit of a man with a dream. I wouldn't be surprised if this guy gives up on politics, loses the will to live, and moves to New Brunswick.

And to you Americans reading this, don't shoot your terrorists. Do as we do in Canada. Have your government treat terrorists like ordinary citizens — ignore them! In good time the bastards will get bored and surrender.

PART IV

Politicians: How Come They Never Listen to Me?

So I Said to
Jean Chrétien . . .

I SAID, JEAN, THERE'S NO INTRUDER IN THE HOUSE, YOU'RE HAVING THAT KEY-
stone soapstone cop dream again.

At 2:23 A.M., Sunday, November 5, 1995, an intruder scaled the
stone wall surrounding the official residence of our prime minister and
his wife, Jean "the Loon" and Aline "the All-powerful" Chrétien.

Surveillance cameras on the wall failed to spot our would-be assassin, because, out of focus and pointing the wrong way, somehow this
guy did not catch his pant leg on one of them.

Mounties have since revealed that for years those same security
detectors have repeatedly been triggered by wind and small animals.
They were quick to note their perfect record in protecting prime ministers from such sinister forces as sudden squalls and chipmunks.

The non-operating cameras did not seriously compromise security because the Sussex Drive RCMP officers were either not there,
asleep at the monitors, or out deer hunting. We're still not sure, since
reports are still being rewritten, and more ass is being kicked and covered than a herd of mules in a hide-tanning barn.

The unidentified intruder approached the residence, and in order
to gain entry, he threw a rock at a ground-level window. The rock
bounced off the window. Okay, so the prime suspect at this point has
to be Dwayne Ward, the closing pitcher for the Toronto Blue Jays.

By taking a bigger wind-up and grunting, the intruder does manage to break wind — sorry, the window — on a second try, and by
flipping a door lock he enters the mansion.

Nobody knows if he wiped his feet; my guess is he did. He's
already shown a great deal of politeness and respect by not cluttering
up the place with a getaway car, not waking anybody up, especially

the guards, and bringing as his weapon of choice a jackknife. The jack-knife is a particularly nasty weapon, in the sense that when you stab something, the blade buckles back, opening a gash in your hand that almost always requires stitches.

Killing may not have been foremost in this man's mind, because the first thing he did was wave at the security camera inside the house. The $10,000 first prize on *America's Funniest Home Videos* may have been foremost on his mind.

At this point, the Chrétiens are awakened by the intruder, and you have to admire a man who, in a tense situation such as this, has the presence of mind to say, "Honey, you go out there. This could be dangerous."

No, he did not say that. When his wife came back and told him there was a lunatic outside in the hallway, the prime minister said, "Ah, that's just Parizeau, the hothead. Fix him a double Scotch and get rid of him."

Meanwhile, Mrs. Chrétien (and yes, we may have elected the wrong spouse in this marriage) coldly slammed the door in the intruder's face, locked it, and called 911. Yes, behind every successful man is a woman in a housecoat slamming doors.

The 911 call set off the secret RCMP response system, which involves carrier pigeons, dog whistles, and decoder rings designed by Disney.

The RCMP response time has been criticized, but I don't think anyone realizes the degree of difficulty involved in saddling up horses when you're half-asleep. And until you find the cassette tape with the Mountie Musical Ride songs, these horses don't budge.

Having had the door slammed in his face, the intruder sat down on a couch in the hall and waited twenty minutes for the Mounties to arrive. He knows there's no point in trying to escape because the Mounties always get their man. But not right away, eh?

Side by side, behind that door, like a painting entitled *Canadian Gothic*, stood our heroine and our prime minister, he in his pajamas and slippers, armed with a .44-calibre soapstone loon, wishing that the heavier, more menacing polar bear had a longer neck for easier wielding.

Fortunately, our prime minister was not charged with possession of an unregistered Inuit artwork.

The intruder is facing four charges, including impersonating a criminal.

In their defence, the Mounties say so many of them responded to the call of duty that even a five-man undercover team was pulled out of the basement of an Ottawa chicken restaurant where they were trying to link Brian Mulroney to the secret Swiss Chalet BBQ sauce.

They say even the RCMP scuba-diving team was pulled out of the Rideau Canal, where they were searching for more boxes of No ballots from the referendum.

You gotta love this country. The Americans may remember the moment Kennedy was shot, but we will never forget the night our prime minister waited behind his bedroom door for a possible assassin armed with a jackknife, poised to conk him on the head with a bird carving.

There's only one way the fiasco at 24 Sussex could have been any more Canadian. And that's if the RCMP, in their rush to get to the prime minister's residence, had to run over a beaver. Not just any beaver, but the original beaver, the one that posed for his picture on the Canadian nickel.

So I Said to Brian Tobin . . .

I SAID, BRIAN, DON'T FIRE ON THE SPANISH FLEET, IT'S BETTER ARMED THAN our navy.

You have to love Canada. (It's not necessarily a voluntary act.) To Bosnia, we sent unarmed peacekeepers. To Chechnya, we sent nasty telegrams. But off the coast of Newfoundland, we eagerly fired upon a Spanish fishing trawler netting turbot, a fish so ugly that when federal Fisheries Minister Brian Tobin announced the species was in danger of extinction, sonar listening devices picked up the sound of other species applauding. This fish is so ugly, some of the baby turbot confiscated from the Spanish *Estai* had little dew worms clipped to their tails so other fish would play with them.

It was a fair fight when it was our navy against their fishing fleet, but if Spain escalated the war to include their ferry boats, we'd be sunk.

So I said to Brian, don't use bullets, we'll bring them to their knees with a dirty-tricks campaign. And here's what we can do:

• Show Canadian Airborne Regiment hazing videos on Spanish television.

• Ruin Spain's tourist industry with a massive ad campaign informing the Brits: "Canada Serves English Fish & Chips Too."

• Compete head-on with Spain's national sport by having skinny Canadians wearing Mickey Mouse hats stab to death large bovine-like animals on Sunday afternoons.

• Initiate a trade embargo of Spain to cut off their supply of black berets and gold teeth.

• Air shocking and graphic videos that show the trees the Spanish use to make olive oil are not, in fact, virgins.

• Anchor pirate radio stations in the water around Spain and play "I's The Bye," twenty-four hours a day.

• Send Spain all the artificial limbs worn by vets of the Mackenzie-

156

Brian, King of the Turbot

Papineau Battalion who fought for freedom in the Spanish Civil War.

• Release a medical study linking impotency to short Mediterranean men who eat fish.

• Order a naval blockade of Madrid and don't tell our navy it's land-locked.

• Change the name of Toronto to Torremolinos and attract drunken Scandinavian tourists to our country.

- Send them photographs of our navy that have been electronically doctored to show they carry the very latest in military hardware.
- Insist that Queen Elizabeth temporarily suspend inter-breeding between the Windsors and the King Juan Carlos family.
- Float billboards all around the Grand Banks that read: We'd rather eat shit with the Airborne than turbot with the Spanish.
- Really mess 'em up by sending Jag Bhaduria to Spain as the Canadian ambassador.

I said to Brian, this dirty-tricks campaign may not work and a real shooting war could yet break out, which is why our military must be ever vigilant.

And while we have our navy on full alert in the North Atlantic, why don't we accidentally capture those annoying little islands of St. Pierre and Miquélon.

Let's see how the prime minister of France feels about the "liberation" of these miserable little lumps in the ocean.

Think about it. St. Pierre and Miquélon are cold, fog-enshrouded, lonely rocks in the ocean — the perfect place for Newfoundlanders to vacation without getting homesick.

And if Quebeckers really do feel they must have their own country, hey, we'll give them a choice of two — St. Pierre or Miquélon.

But no, Brian never listens to me.

So I Said to Sheila Copps . . .

I SAID, THANKS, SHEILA FOR THE FREE FLAG — I'M COMING OUT WITH MY hands up.

Recently, Deputy Prime Minister Sheila "The Shriek" Copps, in her role as heritage minister, said that she wants to see one million Canadian flags being waved in this country on our newly created Flag Day. Flag Day, as you know, is yet another day celebrating Jean Chrétien's failure to grasp the Canadian unity crisis.

Creating Canadian unity by waving flags is like trying to eliminate the national debt by writing promissory notes. Neither one will fly.

We've held Flag Day once, a month ago. I think it went well, and as a traditionalist, I say we continue the fine precedent set by our prime minister on this day. I say each of us, with patriotism in our hearts, goes forth and grabs an annoying little geek by the neck and strangles him until he almost blacks out.

I know the demand for Preston Manning and Larry Grossman will be awesome, but we'll hold some kind of lottery, okay?

Sheila, the Betsy Ross of the '90s, specifically said she wanted to see one million flags on the desks of school children by Flag Day next year. I think this is a bad idea. As a former school kid, I think this would just give our children one more thing to shove down Stinky Sloanowski's shorts while he's bent over napping. (I got one whole week in the principal's office for putting my science project on ants down there.)

But if it's pure patriotism we're after here, then I think one million flags is a terrific idea. And here's just a few suggestions what we might do with them:

• Send the very first flag to Alanis Morissette and tell her she's welcome to use this F word on U.S. television all she wants.

- For maximum public exposure here at home, have bikers bolt them on their handlebars as they travel across Canada to gang-war funerals in Montreal.

- Give five flags to every spectator attending an NHL hockey game in Toronto, so those of us at home can't see the Leafs trying to get the puck out of their own end.

- Plant them coast to coast along the track of our national railway, so VIA engineers can finally throw away their maps.

- Embed the entire million flags in the walls around 24 Sussex Drive to keep the intruders out and the Mounties in.

- Put a price tag of $50 on each of the one million flags and use the proceeds to pay Brian Mulroney in an out-of-court settlement.

- Use them in the opening ceremonies at Doukhobor hazings.

- Make it mandatory that every ship leaving the Welland Canal permanently display a Canadian flag, thus giving other countries the impression that we have a navy.

- Send one to every household in Quebec with the inscription, "Thinking about you, always."

- Sell one for display purposes to the National Art Gallery in Ottawa for $7 million.

- Drape them from the roof of the CBC headquarters and call it a final curtain call.

- Weld them to snowmobiles so we can find them in the spring when the ice melts.

- Promise one flag in the window of every doughnut shop in Canada, thus creating a market for 16 million more.

- Send them to Somalia for the purposes of public burning.

- Put them up in all the trailer parks in Florida to agitate the rednecks and cause a vein to burst in Pat Buchanan's neck.

- Mail the whole million flags to households in Spain with the inscription, "Stick this on your fishing pole."

- Use them to spruce up the banks of the Niagara River so nobody can say Sheila, in her previous job, did nothing for the environment.

- Plant them around Toronto's Queen's Park in a winding path to keep protesting groups from cutting in line.

No, no, here's the best idea. Organize a rally in which one million Canadian taxpayers demonstrate in front of Revenue Canada with one million flags.

Make that one million white flags, Sheila. We'll all come out with our hands up, and you can empty our pockets. So that's what I said to Sheila, but no, she never listens to me.

So I said to Mike Harris . . .

In 1970, I said to Mike, "Mark my words, someday you'll become one of the greatest assistant golf pros the province of Ontario has ever had!" At the time, Mike, myself, Rick Sernasie, and Pete Minogue were having a sub-eating contest in a car in front of Mike's (no relation) Submarines in Buffalo, New York.

Life is strange. It turns out I know Mike Harris from my university days. Mike, then and now, is a decent guy who could never say no to a cold beer and a submarine sandwich. I have no idea what kind of a premier he will prove to be, but trust me, Mike Harris will be hell on the banquet circuit. So it turns out I have spent many hours in the back seat of a car with the new premier of Ontario in a non–Hugh Grant–type situation.

I am not at liberty to reveal any more about Mike's wild and double-salami youth, but will if he doesn't phone me one of these days with word of an important overseas posting.

And I'm also a big booster of Mike's "common-sense revolution." Just look at the line-up of his cabinet ministers.

Al Palladini, a car salesman who is now Ontario's minister of transportation. How common-sense can you get — a traffic expert who knows where to find the jack in the trunk of a stretch limo!

And John Snobolen, a grade 11 dropout, is the minister of education. Perfect. Here's a guy who can not only restructure high school but finish it all in his first term.

So I said to Mike, you didn't go far enough. What about a few more common-sense cabinet appointments. Like Roseanne Barr in labour, Eddie Shack in recreation, and Richard Simmons in energy? What's wrong with Dr. Stubbs in health, and Mr. Submarine as the new minister of consumer relations?

But no, Mike wouldn't listen to me.

What I like most about Mike is, he's a man of action. On his first day on the job, the front page of a Toronto newspaper ran the headline, "Harris Says Ontario Is Open for Business" and then right below it, "Toronto Okays Red Light District." Boy, you want to get the undivided attention of President Clinton — Mike's got the answer.

So I said to Mike, legalize the red light district. It's an idea whose time has come. After years of neglect by both Liberals and the NDP, finally we have investment opportunities for the horny!

I said to Mike, support the red light district and you'll eliminate prostitution.

You see, after Mike supports the red light proposal, it then goes to the federal government for approval, and once the feds legislate it, debate it, regulate it, medicate it, and slap on four taxes plus the GST, nobody in this country, including the hookers, will ever want to have sex again.

But no, Mike wouldn't listen to me.

So I Said to Jean, Captain of Team Canada . . .

I SAID, JEAN, FORGET ABOUT NUCLEAR REACTORS ON THAT TRADE MISSION to China, sell those guys the Pocket Candu, "the stiffer picker upper."

Recently our prime minister led a group consisting of nine premiers and 350 business people on a sales junket to China, offering a catalogue of Canadian products, including our Candu nuclear reactors.

All the premiers and the prime minister out of the country at the same time? Didn't it occur to anybody to seal off all the re-entry points and give ourselves a little good-government insurance?

The reason behind this massive trade mission is that Canada is $550 billion in debt and China has 2.2 billion people with wads of yuan to spend. (China's population is growing at approximately the same rate as our debt, a fact that becomes critical later in this story.)

And how much did this delegation hope to come home with? Less than $10 billion in deals. Putting $10 billion towards a $550-billion escalating debt is like attempting a hostile corporate takeover of Colgate Palmolive with money from the tooth fairy.

(I would like to go on record, herein listing other ideas that would eliminate our national debt, which I have offered to Prime Minister Jean Chrétien in the past and he has completely ignored:

• Cod-watching tours off the Grand Banks.
• Rent the Canadian Air Force out for prom nights.
• Send the Canadian Airborne Regiment to mug the Saudis.
• Designate the national debt an official social program and Mike Harris will kill it.
• Turn the debt into a popular television series and CBC will cancel it.

Thanks, at least *you* listened.)

164

So, while 360 of our best business minds were whistling for rickshaws in Hokang, I was sitting here in Wainfleet, having a few beers and solving three pressing problems of the world, two of which have major global significance. Somewhere around my third Sleeman's Ale, I eliminated our national debt, saved thousands of endangered animals from extinction, and put a stop to the world's population explosion.

Follow me, if you will: Our national debt is $550 billion. There are in China's male-oriented society approximately half a billion men. What one thing would every Chinese man pay $1,100 for and in so doing wipe out our national debt?

Come on, think. Think ground-up elephant tusks, powdered rhino horns, minced monkey testicles. China, obsessed with aphrodisiacs, is the world's most voracious consumer of the proud parts of wild animals, many on the verge of extinction because of this senseless practice. Chinese men appear remorseless in their slaughter of beautiful animals, because apparently most male Chinese suffer from "the droop."

Okay, so the answer to the question "What would Chinese guys be willing to pay $1,100 for that they can't get?" is: it up.

I say forget nuclear reactors. Hey, we got Dr. Stubbs! That's our secret weapon.

(I interrupt this story to warn you, threaten in fact, that if I ever find out, in that whole series of credits — Toronto's Dr. Stubbs learning to perform penile implants from China's Dr. Long, who learned the procedure from Beijing's Dr. Dong, all apparently true — if I find out former Canadian cabinet minister Gerry Weiner was somehow involved, or even the former mayor of New York David Dinkins, I swear I will call for a public inquiry into the whole affair, headed up by Ben Wicks.)

The answer to the Canadian deficit and that of Chinese men is simple: penile implant operations performed on a conveyor belt atop the Great Wall of China by a team of Canadian surgeons led by Dr. Stubbs. Patriotically, we'll call this "stand up and salute" surgery. (Think of it as a one-digit mini replica of the Canadian Space Arm and you've pretty much got the picture.)

I did the math. Half a billion flaccid guys times $1,100 per operation equals $550 billion.

Bingo! We're debt-free into the next century.

The name of this new export? What else? "The Pocket Candu — the last reactor you'll ever need!"

Billboards right across mainland China with our slogan: "Hey! Are you just gung-ho to see me or is that a Canadian-made pistol in your pocket?"

In no time at all, we'll have half a billion Chinese guys cavorting across the countryside like drunken Aussies on a brothel tour of Bangkok. (You *know* it's a real place.)

In one shrewd international maneuver, we avoid federal bankruptcy, eliminate the slaughter of endangered animals, and — if the United Nations will throw in a lifetime supply of condoms with the installation of every Pocket Candu — we can work towards ending overpopulation.

Please get behind me, please support me in my efforts to bring the Pocket Candu to the international marketplace. It's Canadian ingenuity at its peak, if you get my drift.

PART V

Out of the Mouths of Men (and a Few Women and a Couple of Kids) . . . Almost Too Weird for Words

Worms, Weddings, and Other Weird Complaints at the Better Business Bureau

Y OUR LOCAL BETTER BUSINESS BUREAU IS A CLEARINGHOUSE OF CONSUMER complaints. Funded by Canadian businesses, there are hundreds of such bureaus in this country trying to keep you from being ripped off.

These bureaus receive calls about defective worms (too lumpy), drunk disc jockeys at weddings (too jumpy), deep-fried cockroaches in take-out food (also too lumpy), and one from a woman who wanted them to control her daughter's "pet buying habits." Yes, there's nothing worse than an impetuous woman with credit cards loose in a pet shop.

In most cases, the calls that the Better Business Bureau people get are clear and manageable. Some, however, must be submitted to the weird communication decoder device. Here are a few such consumer complaints.

One man called to say his guinea pig had hemorrhoids.

One woman called a furnace company to say she wanted to get her ducts cleaned and the receptionist referred her to a reputable taxidermist. (The receptionist was new.)

One customer bought a dog, then wanted to return it because it growled. (Well, if anybody here has a reason to be irritable and growl, I believe it's the pig with hemorrhoids.)

One man called requesting "cow removal," but emphasizing the fact that there was no hurry to move Ol' Bessie. "She can stay there until the spring thaw," he said.

A woman called to complain because the pet store had sold her a female dog with a penis. The manager stated that the dog did not have a penis when it left the store, but he refunded her money anyway. (I know what you're thinking: Why did she ever bring it back? Imagine, the only one-dog breeding kennel in the world!)

In recording the complaints, the people at the bureau get some rather unusual quotes.

Said one woman, "My father was drunk when he signed the contract, so is it still binding?" (No, the contract is pretty loose; it's your old man that's tight!)

One man who paid a magician to appear at a kids' party complained, "He didn't show up. He just took the money and disappeared!" (Thus saving you the agony of card tricks.)

One woman, without even a greeting, began, "I've got bad gas. And I know my gas because I've had bad gas before." (To cover all the bases, I think you should request a serviceman from Consumers Gas to come to the house and in the meantime take two good hits of Beano.)

One unhappy customer yelled, "They misled me. They committed *freud!*" (You know, psychiatrists are only now discovering that Freud should have been committed.)

One woman complained that when her daughter failed to make payments on a loan she'd co-signed, the company garnished her mother's allowance cheque. She wanted to know if this was legal. (If it's garnished with vegetables shaped like little farm animals, apparently it is legal!)

One woman could get a credit only for merchandise she had returned. As she put it, "I gave the item back to them, but they would only give me a $200 vulture." (Okay, but the high-ticket vulture does hunt rabbits.) Said the staff at the Better Business Bureau, "We think she meant voucher, but around here, you never know."

Some complaints to the bureau are just downright bizarre.

One man claimed a cleaning store was holding his pants for ransom.

One woman complained that her driver's licence photo was ugly, and a man phoned to say that photos of him came back from developing way too "happy." "Not even my kids wanted them," he said. (Trade some "happy" photos for some "ugly" photos and can romance be far behind?)

One customer complained about his new diet plant. "They told me it works like acupuncture," he said. "You put it in your ear." (That would be the second thing you took in the ear, sir.)

Another caller wanted to know if there was a conspiracy amongst Dickey Dee Ice Cream drivers who always hide his favourite flavour in the bottom of the cart. (Some people wonder if there's life on other planets or how viruses mutate. To date, the Raspberry Ripple conspiracy has not captured the national conscience.)

Another older gentleman walked into a bureau office and demanded to know why his horoscopes are always accurate. He wanted to know how these people knew this information about him. (Why don't we just give him the home address of the Dickey Dee paranoid and see if these two problems pretty much take care of themselves.)

One customer got into a heated argument with a furniture salesman about a restocking fee. As she left the store, the salesman gestured at the woman by grabbing his private parts in a lewd manner. (Okay, but was he wearing a military uniform and singing "Beat It?")

Please, the next time you have the occasion to call your Better Business Bureau, speak slowly and with sympathy.

The Better Business Bureau's new motto: Working Hard Every Day to Try to Figure Out What the Hell You People are Talking About!

Canada Customs: The Front Line of Funny

I HAVE NEW AND PROFOUND RESPECT FOR OUR CANADA CUSTOMS INSPECtors. I spoke to one, then another, and after canvassing four border entry points, compiled a series of exchanges experienced by our frontline uniformed inspectors.

Nine out of ten people coming into this country give the officers the information and respect they expect and deserve. It's the one in ten that has our border-crossing patrol people biting their fingernails right down to the knuckles. These are actual questions, answers, and exchanges told to me by customs officials who'd rather sit on traffic cones than have their names appear in these pages.

Officer: "And the purpose of your visit to Canada is pleasure?"

American man, immediately and straight-faced: "Oh, no. I'm on my way to visit my mother-in-law."

Customs officers can count on a variety of cool answers from the after-hours inebriated crowd.

Officer: "Where do you live?"

Young tongue-thickened man: "Fishhook."

Officer: "Fishhook?"

Kid: "Yeah, Fishhook. It's at the end of the line, stupid."

Officer: "Okay, pull over."

Such childishness from today's kids, obviously unable to handle their alcohol. Why, when we were coming back from over the river, ripped and underage, our standard response was Balls Falls. (This actually exists in Niagara!) Balls Falls? Yeah, it's near Pecker's Point. Okay, pull over.

Officer to an American who said he was coming over to his cottage in Canada: "What's the length of your stay in Canada?"

American: "Not too big. Maybe thirty feet by forty."

An exchange at Windsor's Ambassador Bridge:

Inspector: "What are you bringing into Canada?"

Oriental man: "Some poo."

Inspector: "Some poo?"

Driver: "Yes, some poo."

Inspector: "And that's for fertilizer."

Driver: "No, it's for washing hair."

Also from Windsor, the tunnel this time: A man explaining why the floor of his car was covered with marijuana seeds told a customs officer, "I had the window down and they blew in from the expressway."

A man found with several hunks of hash in his underwear at a Niagara Falls bridge told the woman at customs, "I don't know how they got there. These aren't even my underwear!"

Customs officers field a lot of questions from tourists coming into our country.

Woman: "Excuse me, are you a Canadian?"

Officer: "Yes."

Woman: "No, I mean a Royal Canadian."

Answer the officer wished he could give: "Yeah, maybe you saw my picture in the paper recently. I was sucking Sarah Ferguson's toes."

Officer: "How long will you be in Canada?"

American man: "Just a couple of hours. Say, we're just going to drive around the Gaspé Peninsula. You couldn't recommend a good restaurant where we could stop for lunch, could you?"

Wished-for answer: "Yeah, the Lobster Pot in Halifax. At the rate you're travelling, it's only five minutes out of your way."

Tourist: "Does Ottawa have a capital?"

Answer: "Yes, and if it's the Ottawa River, you capitalize both the O and the R."

Many ask about the confusion over miles and kilometres. Some get right to the point.

American: "How fast do your speed cops go?"

Answer: "If they've got automatic speed-wind on their radar

cameras, they can do 200 clicks a minute."

Tourist: "How much liquor can I drink in Ontario?"

Answer: "All you want, if you're a millionaire."

And the old favourite: "Would you speak a little Canadian? The kids would get such a kick out of it."

Customs officials also get a lot of questions over the phone. Believe it or not, the most common is: "What is the most satisfactory method of smuggling goods across the border?"

Hey, you might as well give it a shot!

Question: "If I bring my dog into Canada, do I need a birth certificate for him?"

Answer: "Heck no. A driver's licence and two pieces of photo I.D. are fine."

Question: "When may I be sure the customs officials are not on duty at the border?"

Answer: "July 1, Canada Day. We close the whole damn country down."

You're probably asking yourself: Do customs authorities meet some strange characters in their line of duty?

Well, that depends on your definition of strange.

• King Edward VI driving up in the middle of the afternoon? Buck-naked?

• A 200-pound, four-foot-tall gogo dancer named Twiggy?

• Saint Peter on a freezing night in January wearing only a robe and carrying a bed roll? (They turned him back when they found a loaded .45 in the bed roll.)

• A woman who showed up constantly claiming to be Pierre Elliott Trudeau's date, asking directions to his house? (They turned her back. She'd only have to wait in line once she got there.)

Strange? Constantly, they had a woman show up at a Niagara Falls bridge claiming Brian Mulroney was the Agent of Satan and she was going to Ottawa to do God's work. (Oh sure, back then she was a nutcase. Today she'd be a visionary.)

Niagara Falls Tourists: If You Don't Ask, It Would Be Better for Everybody

Here I would like to answer some pressing questions asked by American tourists when they visit Niagara Falls. Niagara Falls is, of course, Canada's premier phenomenon of nature. If you haven't been there, just imagine the Grand Canyon impersonating a flush toilet.

Every spring and summer, Niagara Falls attracts more than 10 million vacationers from around the world who come to marvel at this spectacular hole in the ground, and when they can't see it, because it is now permanently surrounded by a forty-foot-thick wall of Japanese tourists, many of them jump to their deaths.

These are actual questions recorded by the staff of the souvenir shop at the beautiful Table Rock Restaurant overlooking Niagara Falls. I have inserted the answers they would like to give if they weren't so darn fond of their jobs.

Q: Your coins are lighter than our American coins. Are they hollow?
A: No. They just seem lighter because compared to yours, they're worthless.

Q: How high does the mist go?
A: Way, way, way, way up.

Q: Do you sell film?
A: Yes.
Q: Does the film fit American cameras?

A: It does as long as you have a 110-volt adapter. Just plug your camera into a wall socket when you get back to your motel room.

Q: (Same lady holding a Canadian two dollar bill) Are these Niagara Falls dollars?
A: Yes. They're only valid in souvenir shops. In this country, if you go to a hardware store, you'll need Canadian Tire money, and to buy beer you'll need Beer Store bills. Why don't you just give me all your cash

and I'll write you a note of credit so you can use it everywhere in Canada?

Q: Can we walk to Expo in Vancouver from here?
A: You can, but you'll want to get up real early and pack a lunch.

Q: Do you have any information on the economy?
A: If we did, do you think we'd actually have to charge you six bucks for beer?

Q: Are you allowed to look at the American falls from the Canadian side?
A: Technically, it's illegal. But as long as you don't report what you see to a hostile foreign government, you should be okay.

Q: These nighttime slides of the falls, are they really taken at night?
A: No, of course not. We take them during the day and then we hire community college graduates to pencil in the black parts. We're damn proud of these kids. Plus, it keeps them off welfare.

Q: We don't have to be handicapped to go through the wheelchair entrance, do we?
A: No, of course not. But if it would make you feel better, it would only take a couple of minutes for me to hobble you.

Q: Do you rent barrels to go over the falls?
A: Here at the restaurant, no. You have to go over to the Dare Devil's Rent-o-Ride booth and ask for Dave Munday.

Q: Why aren't there any seals swimming in the falls?
A: Normally there are, but Canada being a highly unionized country, they only work every other day.

Q: Can we go snorkelling in the whirlpool rapids?

A: Yeah, sure. But watch out for people shooting by in those Rent-o-Ride barrels.

Q: Where are the Indians?
A: Cleveland.

Q: Where is the *Mist of the Mating*?
A: *The Maid of the Mist* docks at the foot of the falls. Most of the mating takes place over on Bridge Street.

Q: Do you have to be between six and twelve to go on the *Maid of the Mist*?
A: Yes, but not in years. The rule is you must be between six and twelve feet in height or between six and twelve kilos in weight per person by Imperial volume.

Q: Am I on the Canadian or American side of the falls?
A: It can be very confusing. A good rule of thumb is: If your money is leaving your wallet at twice the normal rate, you're on the Canadian side. On the other hand, if your money is leaving your wallet at gun point, you're on the American side.

Q: What year were the falls built?
A: The hole itself was dug in the early 1900s by immigrant labourers using only handmade stone implements and plastic explosives. The water fountain feature was added in the spring of 1954, when the entire population of Fort Erie, up river, was struck with dysentery, necessitating three days of non-stop toilet flushing.

Q: When does the rainbow come on?
A: That depends. The rainbow over Niagara Falls has become so famous that many of the colours make appearances at other tourist attractions in the Niagara area. It's just a matter of getting them all together and hoping they get along.

Q: Does the Whirlpool Aero Car go to Buffalo?

A: It did last year, but we caught the guy and he's behind bars now.

Q: Do they speak Spanish to you on the Spanish Aero Car?

A: If it's the Spanish guys on duty, then yes, they will. If it's the Natives' shift, they'll speak Aero to you.

Q: Where do I get the People Motivator?

A: I think you want the People Mover over at the Rapids View parking lot. If not, Canadian Tire sells cattle prods.

Q: Do you have to be dressed to eat at the Skylon?

A: If you're having the buffet, we do recommend it.

Q: Is the Skylon Tower a miniature of the CN Tower?

A: Actually, the Skylon Tower is the son of the CN Tower. What we did was, we brought in a world-famous giraffe breeder from the Toronto Zoo and mated the CN Tower with a world-famous commercial structure in New York City. You may remember, not too long ago, that the earth moved under the World Trade Center in Manhattan. Bingo! That was the day.

Q: Isn't it against the law of gravity for a river to flow south to north?

A: You're right, at least it always has been. But about five years ago, we brought in the Canadian Charter of Rights, put a bunch of marine lawyers on the case, and had the law of gravity reversed.

Q: Do we have to pay for Jenny?

A: No, Jenny goes free every day except Saturday and Sunday. If you have a Randy in your group, the whole damn bunch of you don't have to pay.

Q: What are the Secret Tunnels (meaning Scenic Tunnels)?

A: It's classified information. I could tell you, but then I'd have to kill you.

Q: What time do you shut the falls off?
A: We're a very polite people. What time will you be leaving?

Speeders: More Excuses Than a Kid Without His Homework

AFTER TALKING TO A LOT OF TRAFFIC POLICE, I CAME TO THE CONCLUSION that speeders are mostly men and these guys have more excuses than kids caught without their homework done. There are some excuses all cops have heard.

Like: "I gotta go to the bathroom real bad and if you keep me here, I'm going to go all over the front seat."

Or: "I gotta go to the bathroom and it's better to speed than pull over and do it in the ditch."

Or: "I'm not from this area so I don't know how fast I was going."

Or: "I didn't think you were stopping speeders today."

And my favourite: "It's okay, officer, I live on this street." No problem, eh? Like, all those people bouncing off my bumper are friends of mine.

Then there's the Ben Johnson defence: "I wasn't speeding. This car just looks fast."

Or the double-jeopardy excuse: "I already got one ticket today. I didn't think I could get another one."

Then there's the shift-the-blame excuses: "I'm late to pick up my kids at daycare and I have bad kids."

"I had to pass the other car fast. I think he was drunk."

Police never get tired of: "I'm late for court." Okay, here's your ticket and a second chance to be punctual.

And the most common excuse: "My [blank] got stuck."

Police say you can pretty much insert anything you like in that blank — carburetor, speedometer, gas pedal, brain, cigarette lighter, lower torso, clutch, gear shift. They've heard 'em all.

Said one speeder: "My cruise control malfunctioned. Boy, we're lucky this is the worst thing that happened."

Yet another: "You can't know how fast I was going. My radar detector didn't even go off."

A guy stopped for doing 90 in a 50 km zone said: "I'm in a hurry to get new tires because I almost got in an accident last night when I slid and lost control of the car."

Claimed one driver: "My wife is pregnant." When the officer offered to drive them to the hospital, the driver responded: "Oh, no. She's not *that* pregnant."

The emergency excuse I like the best was given by the driver who said: "Sorry, officer, but I gotta get to the hospital fast." When the policeman asked him what the problem was, he said, "It's a private matter. I'm not allowed to discuss it."

On the outskirts of Toronto, a speeding driver was stopped and, pointing a finger at the woman next to him holding a map, said that she was reeling off the street names too fast. He was just trying to keep up with the directions.

Some excuses are once-in-a-lifetime events. Speeder: "I'm having an asthma attack and I have to get home to my puffer." Officer: "How can you drive if you can't breathe?" Speeder: "Well, I'm not dying."

A young man was caught speeding at almost twice the limit. He claimed he had to speed because he was almost out of gas. The officer asked him why he didn't drive slow and conserve fuel. He replied: "Oh no, what I do is go as fast as I can, then put the car in neutral and coast."

You gotta wonder what a guy like that does when he's running low on groceries.

One officer stopped a speeder in downtown St. Catharines, Ontario, and asked him: "Where are you going in such a hurry?" Said the driver: "The Dominican Republic."

Another resident of St. Catharines was stopped and asked if she knew how fast she was going: "No," she said. "I've got cataracts and I can't see the speedometer."

Oh yes, women speed too.

"No. Heaven can't wait, dammit!" Essentially, this was the defence offered by Angela Heavens who was charged with travelling 157 kilometres per hour on the 100 km/h Highway 401 near Brockville, Ontario. Angela had to go real bad. So bad, in fact, she whizzed — sorry, she blew by a service station, driving so fast she failed to see it.

A justice of the peace accepted Angela's emergency call of nature excuse, but later a real judge overturned it stating: "Needing to go to the bathroom falls short of satisfying that test of necessity."

Boy, don't you hate it when someone uses the words *satisfy* and *necessity* when you've got your legs locked together like a twin pretzel?

Heavens was fined $300, the same amount of money (I'm guessing) that she would have been willing to pay to use a roadside portable on that particular day.

This is the one excuse you rarely hear from guys, but police hear it more than you think: "My breasts are killing me." "Pardon?" "I'm breast-feeding and I have to get home and feed my baby before they explode."

And finally, one officer in Eastern Ontario pulled over a speeding car with six occupants and the thing that caught his eye was five of them were hanging out the windows as the car sped by his cruiser.

When he finally got them pulled over, they all immediately bolted from the car, except the mother, who was still in the car, busy changing the diaper of the baby she was holding.

Remember: Speed kills, and speeding excuses just slay the people back at the police station.

The Funeral Business: Funny to the Last Drop

I WOULD LIKE TO DRAW YOUR ATTENTION TO THE HEALTHIEST AND LIVELIEST industry in North America: the death business.

Recently, I spoke to a branch of the Ontario Funeral Service Association, and in the audience was the ever-smiling face of a casket salesman, my old friend — wait for it — Bill Sleep. I'm not making this up.

Before I got up to speak, the group coordinator (nickname "Digger") asked me if it would be all right if they got the business segment out of the way first. I agreed.

I'm not sure if you do any public speaking, but usually it's a good idea to keep things light and entertaining, and in the case of a humorist like myself, funny, if possible. I'm not accustomed to having somebody warm up the crowd for me, so you can imagine my surprise when four gentlemen stood up and briefed the audience on the latest mock-disaster exercises (they went well), new and innovative coffins (they go down well), and the latest in graveyard hydraulics (you go down well). Essentially, they touched on every aspect of death, destruction, and near-annihilation, all of which — if I heard right — are going very, very well.

By the time I addressed the group, my first duties were to get two ladies in the front row to stop crying and physically remove measuring tapes from two competing morticians who were stalking a waiter with a bad cough.

It was the most interesting situation I've ever encountered as a speaker. So much so that I gave the four gentlemen who preceded me a list of my upcoming engagements in hopes that somehow they could arrange to be in another country on those dates.

Do not for a moment, however, think people in the funeral business do not have a good sense of humour. Far from it. In fact, I did a little research into the subject and was able to relate to them some of the lighter moments of the business of darkness. Like actual epitaphs, carved in stone by their colleagues, both here and south of the border.

From a cemetery in Innisburg Falls, Vermont: "Here lies the body of my daughter Anna, Done to death by a banana. It wasn't the fruit of the thing laid her low, But the skin of the thing that made her go."

On the headstone of a Canadian atheist: "Gone to see for myself."

One epitaph that many of us might laugh a little too hard at: "View this dreary spot with gravity. A dentist is filling his last cavity."

On the memorial of a man bitter to the end: "Talked to death by friends."

I am assured by Father William Parker Neal, who lives in Gettysburg and has written a book on epitaphs, that there is a tombstone in his own hometown that reads: "Here lies the body of my daughter Charlotte, Born a virgin, died a harlot. For 16 years she kept her virginity, Which is quite a record in this vicinity."

And two warnings by women about their own funeral arrangements:

Said one: "There will be no male pallbearers. Since they wouldn't take me out when I was alive, I don't want them to take me out when I'm dead."

Said the other: "Please don't let them put 'Miss' on my tombstone. I haven't missed as much as they think."

But, it is most definitely not the morticians who reveal the funny side of the funeral industry. It's the people like you — under the great stress of a loved one lost, yet exuberant in the appreciation of those who have helped you through it. The best, albeit unintended, humour in the death business lies in the thank-you notes people send to the managers of funeral homes.

"I wish to thank everyone who kindly assisted in the death of my husband."

"Thank you for providing the pallbearers for Mom. She always loved to have men help her."

"Thank you for helping cremate my father. It was a pleasure."

"When you returned mother's clothes, the shoes were not hers, but they fit me. Thanks again."

"Thank you for talking me out of burying my husband at sea. Now I can visit his grave. You see, I can't swim."

"Thank you for mother's beautiful funeral service. She was a saint and a virgin if there ever was one."

"Thank you for conducting such a lovely service for my father. The guy who did the flowers was a little too happy, if you know what I mean. But everything worked out okay."

Said one woman to a funeral director: "Boy, I've been trying to settle this estate for nearly a year now. There are some days I wish Harry had never fallen off that ladder!"

You might as well laugh. As Red Skelton has so often said, "Nobody's getting out of this one alive."

Who Needs Comedy Clubs? We Have Schools

ART LINKLETTER IS BACK IN BUSINESS; I HEARD HIM ON THE RADIO THE other day. Ages ago, Art Linkletter had a hit television program entitled *Kids Say the Darndest Things*. Spinning off the TV show with books, albums, and a speaking career, he became a millionaire by listening to what children say. Apparently no kid ever said: "What's my cut, Mr. Linkletter?"

But Art was right — out of the mouths of babes come real beauties. And parents too, especially in their notes to teachers. Somebody sent me this list of excuses American parents included in notes to teachers explaining the absence of their kids. It's compiled by Knight-Rider Newspapers.

(Warning: The material contained within this listing may indicate that these parents have the same reasoning ability and attention span of an O.J. juror. Any similarity is purely coincidental.)

Here are but a few:

- "Please excuse Blanche from jim today. She is administrating."
- "Please excuse John from being absent on Jan. 28, 29, 30, 31, 32, and also 33."
- "Excuse Gloria. She has been under the doctor."
- "Please excuse Jimmy for being. It was his father's fault."
- "My daughter was absent yesterday because she was tired. She spent the weekend with the Marines."
- "Please excuse Sara for being absent. She was sick and I had her shot."
- "Carlos was absent because he was playing football. He was hit in the growing part."

• "Please excuse Ray Friday from school. He has very loose vowels."

Please understand, those were simply errors in written communication. I checked. Nobody got shot, pregnant, or traumatized. Any you'll be pleased to know that Carlos's part did finally stop growing on February 42.

But kids . . . kids is where the real komedy's at. A couple of summers ago, I had the pleasure of hearing Jerry Robinson, head of the Cartoonists and Writers Syndicate in New York, lecture on his *Flubs and Fluffs* comic strips. Jerry Robinson (one of the original Batman artists and creator of the Joker character) did something only a handful of men in the history of civilization have done — he listened to his wife. She was a teacher, he was a cartoonist, and together they collaborated on the weekly colour feature strip that ran for seventeen years in the New York Sunday *News*. Jerry would simply take a real gem that one of his wife's students had mangled on a test paper and create a cartoon around it. Soon thousands of teachers and parents from around the world were sending their favourite true schoolroom boners — up to 1,500 letters a week! These collections were also published.

(Warning: The material contained within this listing may indicate that the kids who made these statements were Macauley Culkin and his brothers after a three-day drunk at home, alone. Any similarity is purely coincidental.)

Here then are a few of those gems:

• The astronauts float around in the cabin of the spaceship due to a state of witlessness.

• In 1588, Spain sent an armadillo to defeat England.

• Magellan circumcised the world three times.

• The garage near our house has an expert maniac on duty twenty-four hours a day.

• The witness refused to talk on the grounds that what he said might incinerate him.

• Crusoe was once shipwrecked on an island, but eventually went on to become a great opera singer.

- In biology today, we digested a whole frog.
- George Washington was one of our original floundering fathers.
- Caesar was victorious in the Garlic Wars.
- Bach had twenty-seven children. He practised on his spinster up in the attic.
- McCormick invented the mechanical raper. It did the job of seventeen men.

The success of Art Linkletter and Jerry Robinson is proof positive — don't be too hard on creative mistakes, especially when they're your children.

PART VI

Geeks "R" Us

The Dumbest Damn Tennis Match Ever Played

It WAS A SUNNY DAY AT THE LAKE, LIKE ANY OTHER SUMMER DAY AT THE LAKE except those that are cloudy, overcast, or fraught with fifty percent chance of precipitation.

On sunny days on Sunset Bay, the guys like to play tennis and drink beer, and for six summers, this combination of honest sweat and icy suds has worked amazingly well. The real key here is not the tennis, which often falls below acceptable amateur standards, or the beer, which can be flatter than a second serve and just as weak. No, the reason why this summer combo of foot faults and froth is such a winner is the order in which we've done it for all these years. First the tennis, then the beer.

Well, on this particular Sunday, Murray the Cop and I got the order backasswards. I don't know how it happened, I just barely managed to remember *that* it happened.

It started with an argument about a volley. I mentioned the term *stop volley* — a short drop shot that ends play because the player in the back court cannot reach it in time to return it. Murray insisted it was a *drop* volley. I declared the terms interchangeable and thus both of us correct. Murray called me a "flippin' know-it-all." I've never known Murray the Cop to be flippant. I suggested Murray was wasting his time as a cop. He'd be more suited to being the poster boy for the Abortion on Demand movement.

What's more, I have credentials. I spent one year in Spain teaching tennis to German tourists in the tiny resort town of Mijas. Even today, if you go to Europe and see Germans hitting ground strokes with crossed eyes, crossed fingers, and yelling "Fore!", that's my handiwork.

My honour challenged, I decided to impart my vast collection of specific volleys to Murrary the Cop as we played. "I suppose you've never heard of a Dolly Volley?" I asked as we changed ends on the odd game. (We changed after every game during this match since all games were odd.)

"What's that?"

"That's the volley hit by a big-breasted woman wearing a blonde wig and singing 'Nine to Five'."

That started it. Thereafter, the volleys flew as if discharged from a stun gun with a bent barrel.

The volley you hit at Christmas — a Holly Volley, unless Santa Claus himself hit it, in which case it was a Jolly Volley.

The shot you hit with a parrot on your shoulder — a Polly Volley.

The one used while performing with Dorothy Hamill in the Ice Capades — a Follies Volley.

Each new volley brought the play to a halt and both Murray the Cop and me to our knees. If you think drinking and driving is a disastrous mix, try tennis on a six-pack and some.

In show business, Lassie would have hit a Collie Volley. Theodore's brother used a Wally Volley on *Leave It to Beaver*, and the Lolly Volley was popularized by Shirley Temple.

In the second set, Murrary apologized for hitting me with a ball by using the Chinese waiter shot, the So Solly Volley, and I thought I heard my shorts rip as I went down on the court.

Somewhere around game four, I rendered Murray immobile with the shot Little Richard made famous — The Good Golly Miss Molly Volley. It took five full minutes for us to get into position for him to serve and me to receive.

As he began to serve, I hit him with the tennis shot two puppets would use in the "Match of Marionettes" — the Kukla, Fran, and Ollie Volley.

Murray missed the ball completely, made a rude noise, and we quit and went home.

I tell you, give us the stage at the Belmont Hotel, a box of beer, one hundred loons just like us, and a fat lady with a hoarse laugh —

Murray the Cop and I would be on the Comedy Channel before you could say "Howie Mandel." The beer ad is right. "It just doesn't get any better than this." The fact is, it just keeps getting worse.

Oh sure, go ahead and have a real good laugh at the expense of a couple of guys who sometimes get a little confused. That's fine. But just remember, although guys in general may not be too damn smart, we are, however, very . . . very . . . very . . . [Publisher's note: At the time we went to print with this book, Bill was still struggling to finish that sentence.]

Danny: Going Through the Babe Stage

So my brother-in-law Danny, whom I'm very proud of because he left Canada Post to return to school, is back in town.

I remember trying to give him some career counselling before he took the job as a postie. I remember saying: "Danny, don't do this. Show some pride. Repossess toasters for a trust company or smuggle cigarettes in from Buffalo."

But no, the kid wouldn't listen to me. Danny had lofty ideas then. He was driven by a heartfelt desire to do something exciting, something different, something good — something he summed up in words I'll never forget: "Babes can't resist a man in uniform, Bill."

You have to understand that Cliff Claven is his role model in life and the television show *Cheers* is, for Danny, the good book by Gideon come alive.

So for years, there he was in his snappy blue-on-blue uniform, with forty pounds of the nation's most sensitive and vital correspondence draped over his shoulder, standing at a local bar called Skuttlebutt's. Danny was one of the most dedicated posties I've ever seen. In sleet, in hail, in dark of night, he never missed a round.

So he's out of school and I, as unbelievable as this may sound, found Danny a cottage on the lake, free for the entire summer. Honest I did.

Now it's not exactly a "cottage cottage" and it's not really even a "cabin cottage." It's more of a foot locker with windows and eavestroughs. This place would have been condemned years ago, except the health inspector thinks it's the woodshed of the cottage next door. But Danny, who is still at George Brown College in Toronto, hasn't seen it, so I had to do a bit of a selling job to get him to take the place. I don't mean to brag, but I used to be one of the 3M company's best sales reps.

I think it would be great to have the kid up here for the season, and not that I'm counting on it, but if he offered to mow my lawn, look after my cat while I'm away, and help me stain and reshingle my house this summer — well, that would be swell. Otherwise, I'll have the little squatter evicted.

So I sit down with Danny and he wants to hear all the highlights of "this cottage on the lake" or, as he's about to find out this weekend because he's moving in, "this shoebox by the shore." Danny has a pen and a piece of paper in front of him because besides being a stickler for detail, he's got the attention span of fresh-ground cornmeal.

"Danny," I said, "you're going to love this place. It's right on the water." I neglected to mention that with a stronger than average north wind, this crate will be *in* the water.

And Danny wrote down: "Babes on the beach."

And I said: "Danny, you won't have any problem with burst water pipes, that's for sure. There's no running water."

And Danny wrote down: "Babes in town with showers in their apartments."

I said: "Danny, you won't have to install any of those annoying little smoke detectors. There's no heat."

And Danny wrote down: "Babes and blankets."

"You sure won't have to wake up in the morning to a mess of dirty dishes in the sink, Danny," I said. "There's no kitchen."

And Danny wrote down: "Babes and take-out Chinese food."

"No siree, Dan," I said. "The best sleep you'll ever have starts at sundown, because, you guessed it, there's no lights."

And Danny wrote down: "Early to bed, early to rise, babes."

"No sir, Danny," I said, "nobody's going to be waking you up at all hours with toilet flushing. There's no toilet."

And Danny wrote down: "Enough is enough."

So the outhouse caused a bit of a hitch in my sales presentation. That's the problem with young people today, they get spoiled with hi-tech toys like indoor plumbing and there's no taking them back to the good old days.

"Why, when I was a kid growing up in Dain City, Dan," I said before he rudely interrupted me.

"Oh, come on, you're not going to tell me you had to use an out-house when you were a kid?" he said, rolling his eyes.

"Of course not," I said, "but we blew old man Michener's up on a regular basis. And once with him in it too."

"How?" he asked.

"Cherry bombs. You can buy 'em in Buffalo."

"Who?" he asked.

"Well, let's say you invite your father out for a few beers and when he has to go to the john . . ."

And Danny wrote down: "Entertainment."

So it's all settled. He's moving in this weekend. I got his confirmation letter this morning: "Hi neighbour: I'll be over every morning for coffee, Danish, and the john. Please have a key made for me as you may not always be home when I need to shower, read, put a fire on, or host a dinner party. Babes . . . can't count on 'em, Bill. Sincerely, your brother-in-law Danny."

He also included a recent x-ray proving that, after all those years of hauling tons of junk mail, his back is so screwed up he can't lift anything heavier than my wallet.

I'm starting to remember why my sales manager at the 3M company kissed me on both cheeks when I told him I was leaving.

Danny's letter ended with: "P.S. — Got my dad coming up to the lake Sunday, need four clusters of cherry bombs and a set of bleacher seats as soon as possible."

Heinz, the Handyman from Helsinki

I KNEW HEINZ ONLY BY REPUTATION: HE WAS A HARD WORKER, AN HONEST man, and he knew how to build a sauna. At the time I hired him, I had no idea that in less than a month I would seriously consider killing this man with my bare hands.

It was September and I had just received payment for the first draft of a television movie. I was rich. As a writer, I get rich about once or twice a year when I sell a script or get an advance on a book. Shortly thereafter, I go through long periods of being poor until I sell another script or get an advance on another book. Hey, it still beats anything you have to put a suit on to do.

Instead of depositing the cheque in the bank and three months later cursing the minus signs on my monthly statement, I decided to build something that I could touch and smell and sweat my assets off in — a cedar-lined sauna.

Enter Heinz, a bull of a man, obstinate, energetic, well over seventy with a slight Scandinavian accent and a true gift for carpentry. He also flirted with all the women in my neighbourhood. Heinz gave me an estimate on what the materials and his labour would cost. It far exceeded the cash I had on hand, but I could dramatically cut the costs by first scaling back the size of the sauna and then working alongside Heinz as his helper.

Working with Heinz would become known in my *How to Build a Sauna* booklet as mistake No. 1.

When I decided to switch the plans to a smaller sauna, I foolishly assumed that because the whole thing was my idea and I was putting up the cash, I was also the boss. Not a chance. I can honestly say that from the first cut of a two-by-four to the final nail in the sauna's door,

199

Heinz never listened to one damn word I said.

My rough measurements would have given me a simple two-person sauna. We built one that seats six, eight in a pinch, and yes, pinching is prohibited. My plans called for a rough wooden floor. I have a tiled floor with a catch basin. I had ordered a small electric heater, cancelled that, and moved up two sizes to the heater I needed for the larger cubic space. I wanted a low ceiling with a single sitting bench. I got a high ceiling with two tiered benches.

The only time during the construction that Heinz solicited my opinion was on the benches. "You want a three-foot bench or a four-foot bench?" he asked one day.

"The three-footer," I replied instinctively.

"You'll be sorry," he said, as he kept working.

You had to abide by Heinz's rules of conversation or he clammed right up.

"Why?" I asked, obediently.

"Well," he said, "I built my niece and her husband a sauna at their cottage up north and they insisted on three-foot benches."

Silence. My cue to say: "And golly gee willickers, Heinz, what happened then?"

"A month later I had to go up and replace them with the four-foot benches," he said.

"Why?" I asked.

"Ah, they have sex on them," he said, and then asked me to pass him the level.

I can tell you in all honesty, I insisted on the three-foot benches and, you guessed it, today I have four-foot benches in my sauna.

As Heinz's helper, I got as much respect as Saddam Hussein's food taster.

I'll admit, I'm not very handy around the house. Every fall I have to hammer a long nail into the top corner of a door in the back of my house to stop a noisy and chilling draft from whistling through it. Twice in six years, I've managed to break the glass in the door while doing it. I'm the kind of guy who can hurt himself just going through the Yellow Pages to find somebody to properly do a job around the house. My plumber, John Balaban, charges me 50 percent less if I promise not to help him.

But Heinz's appreciation of my skills bordered on the abusive.

"I said a ballpeen hammer," he'd yell, "not a hammer and a ball-point pen!"

Maybe it was his accent I wasn't understanding.

"I said six two-by-fours, not four two-by-sixes," he'd scream. "You want I should write this stuff down for you?"

After shop, math was my biggest downfall.

"That's not a nail, that's a tack," he'd say.

"This is a nail. See? It's longer than the board it's gotta go through."

And for all this verbal humiliation, I was paying him $15 an hour.

But the best was our little adventure to Buffalo, because no cedar in the country of Canada was good enough for a sauna built by Heinz.

Heinz sprung the idea on me at noon on a Saturday. It would take about two hours, he said, if we left right away. I was wearing longjohns clearly visible through the holes and tears in my working jeans, a jacket splashed with mud, and a Danny Zack ball hat. I hadn't shaved in days. But when Heinz says "right away," there's no debate, only the expected response: "Yes, mein Führer!"

Even if it took three hours, I'd have time to nap and then put the tuxedo on for a charity auction I was hosting on local cable television at six.

Thirty minutes later, I was bumping along a freeway in Buffalo in the cab of Heinz's mostly homemade truck, being lectured on the evils of the modern world, the solutions to which always involved the flogging of a public figure.

The Busy Bee building materials outlet was exactly where Heinz said it would be, only closed. The union Heinz belonged to (I believe it was the Finnish Fascists for Public Flogging) required that we frequently stop for coffee and doughnuts and that I, the employer, pay. Heinz must have been in a good mood, because he made an exception in his rules for world harmony by proposing that the owner of Busy Bee, a private figure, be flogged.

Then it was on to another Busy Bee outlet, and after Heinz had solved four more disasters threatening human existence on earth, we pulled into the building materials depot, which had a parking lot identical to the first store — vacant. Upon closer inspection, I noticed the front doors were padlocked and a nice note had been left behind by the county sheriff explaining the link between Busy Bee and "chapter eleven." Apparently, the Busy Bee chain of stores had been too busy to pay their taxes.

After another break (the coffee and doughnut budget was killing my cash flow) and five major world crises that could be avoided with the sting of a whip in the hands of Heinz, we pulled into another building supply store, this one called Grossmans.

They, in fact, had cedar strips that met with Heinz's approval. They also had a lot of other stuff I didn't know I needed. For Heinz, a building supply store is like a homecoming, and I spent the next hour pulling him away from scintillating conversations about R-40 insulation, thermal-pane windows, and self-threading wing nuts.

As we approached the Peace Bridge to return to Canada, both lanes were crawling bumper-to-bumper with Canadian cars. There went my nap.

Forty minutes later, we entered the Canada Customs inspection building to pay duty on our goods, and it too was jammed with Canadians. Heinz surveyed the scene and then loud enough for everybody to hear, said, "Geez, doesn't anybody work here?" One thing I've discovered over the years is that the energy and efficiency of government employees does not dramatically improve when their work ethic is publicly attacked.

I tried to distance myself from Heinz, but of course he had to stay close to me, to quietly point out which officials he'd have flogged first.

It was 4:30 P.M. and I had precisely an hour and a half to get home to Wainfleet, shower, dress, and dash to a live microphone in a television studio in Welland.

I bypassed the line that was now out the door behind me and begged a supervisor for a minute of his time. I would leave my credit card, I'd sign the blank forms, if only he'd let me leave and have my handyman Heinz see the process through. Somehow, the thought of making Heinz stay behind and pay for his remark appealed to the customs official. I was off and running.

Dodging cars, I jogged my way out of the customs area to the nearest exit, up a hill to Garrison Road and over to Highway 3, the road back to Wainfleet. From there, I hitched and walked my way a mile down the highway.

If only I could get picked up, I might be able to "buy" a ride to

Wainfleet. A guy in a restored T-Bird pulled over, and I was sitting beside him before the car came to a full stop.

After I complimented him profusely on his automobile, I eased into my dilemma. I'm the celebrity host of a charity auction that starts in less than an hour, I began and . . . he pulled over. That was as far as he was going, he said.

Standing on the shoulder of the road, watching the T-Bird disappear, I wondered what I would do, face-to-face with a guy who looked like a serial killer and claimed he was a television host. The best I could hope for was that he didn't report me to the police.

A hundred cars and another half hour passed by the time I got to the Country Cottage Restaurant on the outskirts of Fort Erie. In I went and asked the waitress if she'd call me a cab. She looked at me just like the T-Bird guy did, and she hadn't even heard my story!

I kept hitchhiking while I waited for the cab to arrive. Another thirty cars and ten minutes passed me by. And then I saw it — a beat-up station wagon with a lit-up taxi sign on top. This was my saviour coming down the highway, slowing to make sure I was his fare and not some wild-looking mental patient who ordered a cab from Fort Erie to Wainfleet and promised to pay with cash he said he had in the house and —

"Hey! Hey! Come back here!"

The cabbie got close enough for a good look, pulled a U-turn, and returned to the safety of his taxi stand.

Now it's getting dark and I'm walking and hitching and half-running, when coming towards me I see what looks like an odd-shaped truck that had been reconstructed by an owner who thought he had better engineering ideas than the Ford Motor Company. Heinz!

Good Lord, I swear I never thought I'd be so happy to see this man again.

Heinz, you're a sight to behold! I waved, stepped onto the road, then jumped back onto the shoulder as a car passed Heinz's truck on the inside lane, nearly taking me with it.

Heinz never saw me!

I screamed, I yelled, I waved my arms as Heinz drove away from me, towards home. Of all the figures that needed flogging . . . *Wait! He's pulling over!* The brightness of Heinz's brake lights was the best thing I'd seen since breakfast. Madly I ran for the truck, which was a hundred metres down the road before it finally stopped.

Out of breath, I opened the door and dragged myself up onto the seat. I was gasping for air, unable to talk. And as I sat there heaving, I hear the slightly accented voice of Heinz say: "You're a lucky boy today."

And as I turned to look at the man I was paying $15 an hour to abuse me, to drink coffee and eat doughnuts, to turn my leisurely Saturday into a hitchhiker's horror story that Stephen King would approve of — he said, with a slight laugh, "I don't usually pick up hitchhikers!"

The next time you look at the photo of a convicted killer, please, don't say, "Gee, he doesn't look like a murderer!" Trust me, all of us, under certain circumstances, are capable.

I did get to the charity auction, late. And I did end up with a sauna, Heinz's. Right down to the lock on the door that I didn't want but now have, Heinz built me the sauna of *his* dreams.

And as much as I hate to say it, the man was absolutely right. I'd have tired of the tiny sweatbox I had in mind and eventually lost interest in it.

I now have a beautiful cedar-lined spacious sweat room where I spend many relaxing hours each week.

Near the end of the project, I was running out of money. Heinz wanted to put a wooden railing around the heater for safety's sake. I said no. By this point, I'd been using the sauna and there was no safety problem. He was either being overly cautious or padding his worksheet. Either way, I insisted a railing not be built. And for once I got my way.

A week later Heinz came by to pick up his tools and I had a slight change of heart. As casually as I could, I broached the safety factor. "Listen, Heinz," I said, "that railing you mentioned around the —"

"You burned your ass on the heater, didn't you?" he blurted out, before bursting into what passes in Finland as laughter.

"I did not. No way. I did not burn my ass on anything, I just thought . . ."

"Then drop 'em. Go ahead. Pull 'em down and show me!" he dared.

"Geez," I said, "you're even weirder than I thought. Just put a railing around the sauna."

"Maximum — one hour's work!" I yelled as I left him standing there laughing.

Don't think for one minute I didn't have the nerve to drop my drawers. In fact, it would have been a fitting end to our relationship.

And I would have, too, except the burn on my bum was so fresh, the blisters were still sticking to my underwear. Honest — it happened just like that.

The Unabomber, O.J., and Me

THE UNABOMBER IS DOOMED TO DIE.

I've been following the case of the Unabomber very closely, and I'm afraid the man doesn't stand a chance.

His Montana cabin full of bombs, bomb-making equipment, an original of his 35,000-word manifesto, and the typewriter used to produce it offers such overwhelming evidence that in accordance with the American judicial system for high-profile cases, trust me, one year from now this guy will be free as a bird and playing golf with O.J. Simpson. And that's when he'll get it.

On one seemingly innocent day, the Unabomber will ignore a one-stroke water hazard penalty, claim he got a four instead of a five and the next thing you know he'll be saying his last words to an agitated dog. O.J. comes down hard on cheaters.

Hey, I'm kidding. The cases of O. J. Simpson and the Montana suspect are totally dissimilar, because if you compare police reports, witness testimony, evidence, motive, and whereabouts, you'll find the Unabomber killed three people, not two.

Of course, the biggest difference in these two cases is that the Unabomber will never be able to produce a video to assert his innocence after he's wrongfully acquitted. Not a chance. Oh sure, many Americans would be tempted to dial the 1-800 number to order it, but who's going to open the package when it comes to the door?

"Honey, save that UPS package for your mother to open on the weekend, okay? It's a surprise."

No, Simpson and suspect Ted Kaczynski could not be more different. For instance, Kaczynski is a Harvard-trained mathematician and O.J.'s alibi is that at the time of the murders he was chipping golf balls, having a nap, taking a shower, and talking to his girlfriend on his car phone — all at the same time.

The FBI agents who raided the Montana cabin and arrested the long-haired unkempt muttering occupant were later surprised to learn that it was the alleged Unabomber and not famed freeloader Cato Caelin.

Had it not been for his brother David, suspected bomber Ted Kaczynski might still be at large, living free in America's big sky country, just down the road from the heavily armed Freeman Militia group, not far from the heavily armed white supremacist neo-Nazi ranch, northwest of the once heavily armed and now burned-out Branch Davidian compound, three states away from the bombed-out building in Oklahoma City.

Hello, America? Hello? You people have spy satellites circling the earth that can read the daily special on the sign outside of Stuckey's. Do you not see a pattern developing here?

When you stand at attention with your hand over your heart singing the words "bombs bursting in air," would not both hands over your head be a more appropriate position to take? First disarm America, then the world.

Anyway, brother David Kaczynski hired a private investigator after he experienced "nagging feelings" about links between Unabomber targets and Ted. The tipoff was, every time David opened a birthday card from Ted, he'd lose a couple more fingers.

Apparently, the United States post office is furious that their delivery system was unwittingly used to help the Unabomber carry out his dastardly deeds. Their position is, if they're going to be a party to any maiming and killing, it should be done by disgruntled postal workers and not some stranger. The postal union has filed a grievance.

And I'm sure you're saying to yourself, well gee whiz, Bill, couldn't we use a Unabomber in this country even if it's just to deliver crucial court documents to Brian Mulroney? Hey, now that would be wrong. And besides, a successful Unabomber could not exist in Canada.

First of all, in the RCMP we have one of the finest national police forces in the world, highly trained in intercepting suspicious mail destined for the leaders of this country. No, in order for a Unabomber to be successful here, he would have to jump a stone fence, break a window, and personally deliver the package to the leader's bedroom.

Second, I'm guessing that if most Canadian males handle their mailings like I do, the market is pretty thin up here for potential Unabombers. I hardly ever lick and seal an envelope for the mail without having to reopen it later to insert something I've forgotten to include. Ripping into your own mailings is a very bad habit for a Unabomber. In that line of work, it's the mistake you only make once.

In the event that the Unabomber reads this and takes exception to it, my publisher welcomes a response, in writing. I said *in writing*. Faxes only, if you know what I mean.

Hundreds of Horses Die for Sport

WHEN IT WAS CONCEIVED IN THE 1860s BY JOCKEYS IN ENGLAND, WATER derby involved playfully passing a ball around in shallow ponds at the racetrack while mounted on their steeplechase horses.

Today, water polo is a tough, demanding sport played in deep pools by both men and women from forty countries, athletes driven solely by the lure of Olympic gold.

This past week at a press conference in Ottawa, London's International Animal Rights group said enough is enough. "Two hundred and two horses drowned in polo pools last year alone and the world, especially the Canadian public, should be ashamed of themselves," said Samuel Steed, spokesman for the group.

Steed went on to say that horses drowning in the sport of water polo used to be a rarity, but now that it's an Olympic event, gold medals and large endorsement contracts are pushing the players to raise their game to another level, which means keeping the horses under the water longer.

Steed claimed that of the 202 equine fatalities last year, 120 were at the hands of Canadian polo players, and 92 of those by the women's Olympic team. "Let's face it," said Steed, "women simply do not have the lung capacity of male athletes. They need to come up for air more often. In order to keep the ball moving towards the opponents' goal, they keep the horse's head under water longer, sometimes for the entire length of an offensive charge."

By comparison, Steed produced statistics that show Hungary, the number-one water polo country in the world, did not have a single pony perish in 1995. "How many polo ponies must die in the pools at the hands of desperate Canadian females before we ban this sport entirely?" asked Steed, who was near tears at this point in his address.

London's International Animal Rights staff say their protests have been ignored by Olympic officials in Atlanta where construction has been completed on the new 15,000-seat Aquatic Center.

"Ted Turner and Jane Fonda have box seats on the fifty-yard line complete with a wet bar, while the ponies are kept in cages out in the parking lot in the hot sun. I think this is bloody unfair!" said Steed.

In his last campaign to save animals, the British activist forced the County of Kent to fence off the cliffs of Dover to slow the suicide rate of lemmings.

Steed shocked the room of mostly reporters and humane society officials when he revealed that horses who drown in saltwater pools are being sold for meat on the European market. "The saltwater acts as a tenderizer and a preservative, fetching a higher than normal price in Europe," said Steed. Entrecote is quite a delicacy in Europe.

An angry Susan Fulhearn of Water Polo Canada said she personally knew nothing about selling horse meat for food. Under questioning by Steed, she did, however, admit that water polo's budget had been cut to $70,000 last year by Sport Canada, and that they were looking at a variety of fundraising schemes.

Ms. Fulhearn articulated the main financial problem with water polo: since most of the action takes place under water, spectators have no interest in paying to sit in the stands and seeing nothing. Except Norwegians, she said.

When asked if she personally had ever eaten horse meat, Susan Fulhearn stomped out of the meeting room.

Steed proceeded to introduce two medical officers from Lapland, the only country Canada managed to beat last year, who appeared to verify his claims. Doctors Eurt Ton and Loof Lirpa, veterinarians from Lopphavet, produced photos of horses on stretchers and ambulance drivers wearing tiny Canadian Maple Leaf pins, purportedly given to them by Canadian polo players to buy their silence.

It was at this point that the press conference turned into complete mayhem.

Everyone, even water polo officials, was alarmed when Susan Fulhearn stormed into the Eugene Whelan Room of the Château Laurier Hotel riding Glug Glug, the lead pony of the women's team. Although Fulhearn planned to show that there was no sign of animal mistreatment, Glug Glug, startled by the camera lights, evacuated loudly near the speaker's podium and the whole place cleared out.

Out in the hall, Samuel Steed said poor sanitation in the pool was another reason to ban the sport. Susan Fulhearn, returning to the room with an armful of paper towels, had no comment.

For further information, animal rights supporters can contact the group, London's International Animal Rights (L.I.A.R.) at 1-800-NEIGHHH! or, on the Internet, user/id@williamthomas.wainfleet.on.ca.dot.dot.dot.stay calm.

The Horse's Butt Rebuts

Okay, BACK OFF, PUT YOUR GUNS DOWN, STOP HARASSING MY EDITOR, AND quit asking my mother if she'd consider a retroactive abortion.

Suffice to say, I couldn't be more unpopular these days if it were revealed that I was the illegitimate son of Sheila Copps and Mike Harris. (Get that smile off your face, Sheila, it's just a joke!)

I haven't gotten so much nasty mail in one week since I wrote a piece about breast-feeding in public, and that I'm against it. (For the record, it was in a restaurant and I was jealous that the kid was getting his food instantly while I waited twenty minutes for my bowl of soup. That bothered me. That and the fact the kid was eighteen years of age. But it was in Nova Scotia, eh?)

All right, so let's deal with one story at a time. Concerning the piece about horses dying for sport: would the animal rights activists please stop giving my home phone number to weird people who keep threatening to stake me naked on an anthill in the middle of a mink farm? Please.

I'm only going to say this once. They do not use horses in the sport of water polo. Apparently, I was misinformed.

My research assistant, Debbie Kalender, is dyspeptic, and sometimes the material I request is all ass-backwards by the time it gets to me. Like the time I asked for information on the venetian blind and wound up going to Italy to interview a guide dog.

Mistakes happen. She's a sweet girl who means well. So get off her back, okay?

Besides, anybody with half a brain knows that horses have not been used by the Canadian Olympic polo teams since 1964, when they were replaced by porpoises. No porpoise has ever drowned in a water polo match, and in fact, after their playing days are done many have gone on to star in movies like *Free Willy* and *A Fish Called Wanda*.

Perhaps you read that story but missed the publication date of April 1. This I understand. Since Lopphavet is a real place in Lapland, maybe you didn't question the names of the veterinarians Eurt Ton and Loof Lirpa, which backwards spell Not True and April Fool. That's all right.

But does anybody in a waking state of mind believe a prestigious Canadian hotel would name a ballroom after Eugene Whelan? Please. A truck shop or a mechanical bull bar, maybe. But a ballroom?

Now, about another story I wrote, offering helpful hints for seniors, I just want to say that the hate mail didn't bother me half as much as the photo I received in the mail with my head taped to the body of a ferret and captioned "William the Weasel."

One tip was that senior women may want to sort through their purses occasionally and toss out redundant or expired material. Yes, my mother does carry enough health cards to constitute a euchre deck. No, she is not suspected by the Mounties of being the ring leader in an elaborate scheme to sell state-sponsored gallstone operations to illegal immigrants. I made that up.

And in philosophizing that old age is a time when your conversations get longer while your body gets shorter, I pointed out to senior male drivers that it was not enough for the rest of us to try to spot the knuckles on the steering wheel, that they should wave every so often to let us know they're in there.

Well, seniors, as I said, might be a bit slow, but they're certainly fast off the mark when it comes to hate mail.

From Dennis in Stoney Creek, Ontario: "I would think you are ashamed of yourself, saying all those nasty things about that elderly lady at the checkout. It could have been your mother. She still loved you, even if you may have been the ugliest baby in the ward. Don't forget, you gave her pain when you were born . . . there were times when you filled your diapers with kaka and mom was glad to clean you up."

First of all, I had a little trouble with your handwriting, Dennis, and I'm not sure if the word was "ward" or "world." Secondly, I'm sure I caused some pain at birth, but remember, I wasn't always the size I am today. And finally, Dennis, "kaka"? I believe the correct terminology, sir, is baby poop.

And Betty MacLean, seventy-five years of age, from Egmondville, Ontario, challenged me to a 7:30 A.M. foot race to see which one of us arrives at the Tasty Nu first. I have no idea where Egmondville is, but I'm not stupid. Betty, even if I leave Wainfleet at 6:30 A.M., you'll be in downtown Egmondville before me. The name of the town used to be Edmonton, until the local paper, *The Expositor*, got a new computer with a spell-check feature.

Anyway, if the animal lovers and the seniors will stop referring to me as that part of the horse that crosses the finish line last, I will gladly explain my behaviour because —

(We interrupt this column to bring you a late-breaking, really bad joke from a field in southern England.)

First cow: "So, Irv, are you worried about this mad cow disease?"

Second cow: "Me? Worried? I'm not worried. Why should I be worried? I'm a penguin."

The truth is, I ate beef in England several months ago. I had a steak on New Year's Eve, on the Isle of Wight, and a beef curry in London several days later. Honestly, I thought nothing of it until a few weeks ago, when feeling a bit bloated, I asked the guy who checks my gas meter if he wouldn't mind milking me. I would have loved to have seen the look on this face, but unfortunately I had my head down eating the grass around the well cap at the time.

Just yesterday I skidded into a ditch while chasing a milk truck down Lakeshore Road. I'd have caught it too, except that, as I rounded the Camelot Bay curve, my right front hoof went clean through my Reebok and I spun out of control.

Thank goodness I live in Wainfleet, where this kind of behaviour doesn't attract attention.

So, as to why I wrote those two controversial stories I can only say — I'm mad, I tell you, mad, mad, mad.

I'm not asking for your sympathy. I'm asking for maybe a small bale of hay or even a hunk of rocksalt.

I know you find this udderly preposterous, but that's my story and I'm sticking to it — I have mad cow disease. Please, be patient with me. I'm up half the night regurgitating.

Louie, the Weather Is Beautiful, I Wished You Were Here

AS YOU GET OLDER YOU REALIZE A LOT OF PEOPLE YOU REFER TO AS FRIENDS are really just artful acquaintances. But Louie, Louie I knew would be a friend for life within the first five minutes of meeting him.

Louie Nagy was sixty years old when I met him in the '70s, short, dark, handsome, and Hungarian. A gentle and charming man.

When we shook hands on the tennis court, as we would hundreds and hundreds of times thereafter, Louie bowed slightly, a throwback to his military days.

Louie had gone to his local club to take up the game of tennis, but the two instructors, after giving Louie a couple of lessons, told him to give it up and try bowling. Louie was no quitter. So he came to my club, got some basic instruction from the pro, Dutchy Doerr, and in short order, Louie became very good.

Having taken up the game late in life and being mostly self-taught, Louie had no style. All he could do was win. Louie could paint the lines, as they say, like nobody else — razor-like passing shots placed exactly where the opponent wasn't.

Dutchy and I used to delight in watching hot-shot juniors challenge Louie, big smirks on their faces after watching him warm up. We used to bet on how far they'd throw their racquets at the end of the match.

Louie and I became doubles partners. In one of those what-goes-around-comes-around kind of thing, we got to the finals of an interclub tournament against — you guessed it — the two instructors who had advised Louie to take up bowling.

Yes, justice was served. We won. I wouldn't say Louie was excited, but it's the first time I'd been kissed by a man on a public tennis court.

Louie Nagy was the happiest man I'd ever met. Some days on the court, he'd stop the play, come over to me, and say, "Beel, it's so beautiful today, so good to be here with you." Not only was Louie the only guy I let kiss me, he was also the only person I let call me Beel.

I never knew two people more in love than Louie and his wife, Gyorgyi. Every day, all day, for the nineteen years I saw them together, they were like teenagers with crushes that wouldn't quit.

A framed photo in their dining room taken in the '40s, looked like a Hollywood movie promotion: Louie a dapper Clark Cable lookalike; Gyorgyi, a blonde and more beautiful than a Gabor sister.

Often they would go to Buffalo for an afternoon to sit in the park, listen to music on a transistor radio, and drink pink champagne.

Once, on a very hot day, down by the Niagara River, there were four of us doing just that.

Certain Louie would stop me, I began taking off my clothes to go for a swim. Certain Gyorgyi would stop him, Louie began taking off his clothes to join me. Certain she would fall down from laughing, Gyorgyi had to return to the picnic table to steady herself.

I loved to make Louie laugh. He'd giggle like a kid and then his face would lock in a delirious smile and his body would shake with laughter.

One day Louie proudly drove up in his new Chrysler New Yorker, his "talking car." The automatic voice system would tell Louie to do up his seatbelt and Louie would say, "Thank you." The car would tell Louie to remove his keys before locking the doors and Louie would laugh, do as he was told, and say, "Thank you." He loved it.

That lasted about a week. The next time I saw Louie, he was cursing at the car "Shut up" and "Mind your own business," all while he kicked the tires. I can't tell you the last thing he said to that car the day he got rid of it.

I believe Louie found so much joy in the simplicities of life because he was denied them for thirteen horrific years. The scars of torture on his body never let him forget how fortunate he was, each and every day he was free.

A captain in the Hungarian cavalry, Louie was one of 5,000 men shipped to a Russian prison at the end of the Second World War. He was one of only seventeen to survive.

Gyorgyi was pregnant when he was captured, and thirteen years later he walked into a café in Rudesheim on the Rhine, West Germany, where she waitressed and waited all those years. That's when Louie discovered a dark-skinned, twelve-year-old hellraiser named Attila. This was the son he never knew.

The last few years, a couple of vital organs had been failing Louie, but he'd been making a great comeback. It was time for us to get together, so I wrote down "call Louie" in my daytimer. Busy, I crossed it out and moved it to the next day and did the same the next day.

The next day, Attila called me, and within days it was all over. A lot of secrets died with Louie, but not the secret of happiness.

At the funeral home, it dawned on me that only a person robbed of freedom and dignity could cherish it so much, once it was miraculously restored.

Louie loved Canada, but he laughed at how much we take for granted, how complacent we are in protecting our rights and freedoms. Louie Nagy — 1916–1995.

I don't want to live as long as Louie, just as *well*.